THE ESTABLISHMENT

THE ESTABLISHMENT

A Symposium edited by
HUGH THOMAS

Clarkson N. Potter, Inc./Publisher

NEW YORK

*Printed in Great Britain and
first published in 1959
by Anthony Blond Ltd
34 Beech Street
London E.C.1*

Library of Congress Card Catalog Number: 60—11495

© Anthony Blond Ltd. 1959

Contents

The Establishment and Society

by Hugh Thomas

Historian and novelist. Aged 27. Author of *The World's Game*, *The Oxygen Age* and *The Spanish Civil War* (in preparation).

THE English are accustomed to think of their society as being organized in three classes—upper, middle and lower. On the other hand, many of those who consider themselves members of an 'upper-middle' class (tacitly accepting this ternary classification slightly modified) also make a more stark division: 'gentlemen' and the rest. They thus postulate only two basic groups, enabling them to fancy themselves as belonging to the upper rather than any lesser division of the community.

In truth, however, English society is more complicated: English social groups are not classes in the sense that Roman society was classed into patricians, knights and plebeians. England is composed of a number of violently opposed sections, whom it would be inaccurate and invidious to list in any ranking order. The characteristics of the sections derive not so much from birth, wealth, or profession—though these, of course, play a part: the sections are divided from each other in their political aims, although each group would deny that they were primarily concerned with politics—a word to which they give the too narrow interpretation of being exclusively the play of the political parties. The real sharpness of the hostility of the different groups is obscured, in fact, both by the impulse to classify the nation in social classes and by the two-party tradition. Beneath the façade, however, of the respectable-seeming English democratic institutions, a naked struggle, simply for power, is nevertheless permanently going on between the various groups who care very little for 'democracy' (the formal name of the political organization of the country) or anything which they understand by that conveniently vague word. The only thing which these groups have in common is the assumption which each makes that it alone is the repository of the enduring worth of the nation and also their common reluctance to think in any terms beyond those of the English nation state.

This is especially true of the first group which, for the sake of categorization, I name (perhaps misleadingly) *the Saxons*: these are the large number of tenant and yeoman farmers found throughout the country but especially in East Anglia, Lincolnshire and the West Country. The varied beauty of the countryside itself, the recollection of their successful endeavours in the two world wars to beat the enemy blockade, the continuing use of the image of John Bull to epitomize the typical Englishman, combine to make the Saxons reckon themselves and their own interests superior to all others. They are relatively few in number, but they nevertheless succeed in persuading successive governments that they have a moral obligation, by subsidies and tariffs, to protect Saxon prosperity regardless of any economic criterion. For them, English 'liberties' have nothing to do with freedom of speech or majority votes: the Saxons simply desire that they should be free to continue to be themselves and to make as few compromises as possible with a social or collectivist attitude to agriculture.

The Saxons are assisted in the preserval of their rural isolation by *the agricultural labourers*. They too are only exceptionally collectivist in outlook; their organization in the form of unions is rudimentary or non-existent, they are hardly ever enrolled in professional insurance schemes (whereby industrial workers are in many cases afforded social security). But—largely because the character of their work permits them to preserve their identity as individuals—their relations with their employers are better than labour-relations in industry. They are as nearly concerned to resist change as the Saxons themselves and, if they bother to vote, they often support the Conservative party, which they rightly believe more to represent the past, the changelessness of the changing seasons, the rhythm of the harvest, than the Socialists, who, in England as elsewhere in Europe, are the party of the nineteenth-century industrial cities.

The values and aims of both these sections of society are quite different from a third section whose members often live among them, especially in their declining years: *the Normans*. By this name I refer to the officer class, to the surviving members of the landed aristocracy, or gentry, to certain elements of the public services. Members of this section are peculiarly conscious of their status as 'gentlemen'. They are devoted to the monarch, to the idea of the Commonwealth, and they are the main support of the Anglican church. They are patriotic, though not from a pride in the great tradition of English civil liberties, nor from a glory in the incomparable achievements of English literature and English science, but from a respect for the grave, philistine, disciplined virtues of English gentlemanly behaviour—virtues which, from about 1860 until 1930 (though the Normans appear to suppose the time to have been at least a Julian period),[1] were displayed in all continents of the world and especially in India. When the Normans regret the passing of the British *raj* in India, they are, of course, mourning a power in which the other sections of the English community did not participate and which was their own most brilliant achievement. The Normans have mainly forgotten (if they ever knew), that British world power was built in the first instance by commercial acumen, not the sword—though they personally probably owe their shrinking family wealth to the mercantile prowess of some (usually despised) Victorian forbear. Their anglicanism is the product less of a belief in God (whom they treat rather patronizingly, as if He were the headmaster of their sons' public school)[2] than of a jovial, knowing and smug connivance with the Church: the vicar has an important moderating role in the life of the village, the Archbishop of Canterbury does his bit at the Coronation, the army chaplain can be relied upon to give sensible sermons never going beyond four-letter words. The Normans' favourite topic of conversation is often to curse the Labour Party—whom they believe indistinguishable from, though less successful than, Soviet Communists—and they hardly bother to pay even lip-service to democracy. But they hate business men almost as much as they do the industrial workers, and they therefore enter politics only in order to try and preserve the *status quo* for as long as possible. They will resist every change ferociously but, after it has occurred, they will easily absorb it, perhaps destroying its effectiveness by permeating it from within.

Despite the Normans' dislike of industry and labour, their real enemies, however, are the fourth group—whom it is impossible to call by any other name than *the intellectuals*. They may be

[1] Like the Japanese who, during the same period, were brought to believe wholeheartedly that the Emperor was descended from the sun, many English people are quite unable to grasp the historical fact that many of the traditions of behaviour to which they are so attached were developed no more than three or four generations ago, and in many cases only one or two.

[2] It is surprising, indeed, that no distinguished Norman painter has yet depicted God in the role of chairman of the headmasters' conference.

defined as those who have actually taken their education seriously, and their outlook has been mainly formed by their education. If they do not themselves come from intellectual families, their universities or schools will have given them a respect for things of the mind which is hard to adjust to their own backgrounds. They are to be found in the teaching professions, both at schools and universities, in the Civil Service, in journalism, the liberal professions, and the arts. They are rational in their outlook and are generally still hopeful that they can participate in the development of a better world. They are therefore inevitably at least anti-Conservative, though their dislike of capitalism is often more aesthetic than political. As a group, however, their socialism does not go further than a respect for economic planning and an opposition to imperialism: it is this last which makes them so hated by the Normans, who (again as a group) seem genuinely to believe that, had it not been for 'all this education', the world would be happier, Africa and Asia would be jointly run by a miraculously preserved Cecil Rhodes, and even in England the old pre-Lloyd George order would still be maintained. Geographically, the intellectuals are rarely bred outside London and the university towns. The phenomenon of their existence as a group at all is comparatively recent; for, for a long time, the idea of an English intelligentsia, with standards and habits of their own, was considered impossible, suspect and continental; at present, however, their position, derived from an increasing flow of graduates from the universities who are not, as in the past, inevitably absorbed by one of the other sections of the community, is likely to be become more and more prominent.

The fifth section is *the petty bourgeoisie*. These are all the small business men working on their own, the small shopkeepers, and the lower grades of the Civil Service. Their outlook is static rather than conservative, though their snobbish respect for the Normans, however, leads them to vote for the Tory party. Though without them there could be no capitalism, they have little in common with the sixth group—*the capitalists*—whose importance in the life of the community is so considerable. These comprise both the managers in industry and the financial administrators in the City. Before the Second World War, the City was probably more powerful than industry, but the relationship has now been altered in industry's favour, due to the decline of British world-wide commercial eminence. There is naturally an antagonism between these two sources of power, but hardly so much as would render them two separate groups; for the dominating motive of both remains identical—profit the aim, 'confidence' the means; and, although the City's traditions date from the seventeenth century, its professional attitudes are, like those of industry, those of the great age of English industrial and commercial power, the 'fifties and 'sixties of the nineteenth century. For all the capitalists believe still in the virtues of private enterprise as firmly as did Cobden, and their agreement to state intervention of any kind remains reluctant.

The two remaining groups are also the product of the Industrial Revolution; they are *the English Swedes* and *the Heavy Industrial Workers*. The former group is found mainly in the south: they have been the chief beneficiaries of the Welfare state, and their chief problem is indeed that of a country such as Sweden: now that the great struggle against poverty, unemployment, hunger, disease, ignorance, has been more or less won, how can they construct a society where their self-respect and individuality can be preserved and their creative qualities fulfilled? In the main, the English Swedes are employed in light industry or in concerns with advanced, modern-type machines and facilities; they are alive to the more sophisticated problems of industrial society such as those of centralization, 'incentives', the proper use of leisure. Although a majority of this group still votes for the Labour party, a large minority vote Tory—possibly because the mere act of so doing panders to their desire for social (in the limited sense of the word) advance.

The final group in English society is still the largest single group. The heavy industrial workers are, of course, those workers in the heavier industries who have not yet attained the Swedish heights. They are still wrestling with black, semi-nineteenth-century problems of labour relations, bad conditions, overcrowding in towns. Their socialism is accordingly more old-fashioned: they are interested above all in getting a better share from existing society than in changing it, though the latter will no doubt have to occur to secure the former. They are mainly found in London, in the great industrial towns of North and North-East England, in South Wales and along the Clyde.

These eight groups make up English society at the present

time. Of course, they are less clearly distinguished from each other than is here suggested. On the other hand, most people clearly belong, with regard to what they want to achieve, to one or other of the groups, and everybody belongs more to one group than to another. It would not be surprising, therefore, if the English political scene were cluttered with as many parties as exist say, in Italy, or did exist in pre-Gaullist France. And such a large number of parties would exist in England if we were to enjoy any form of pure democracy. Following continental precedents, the Saxons would no doubt call themselves the 'Peasant party', the capitalists might take the name of Independents, and the intellectuals, the Radicals. One might surmise that the Normans would be led either by a junta of retired generals and dukes. The heavy industrial workers would probably have been inveigled into following the lead of Moscow, and the Swedes would no doubt be socialists of the Mollet brand—easily persuaded of the dangers of an *apertura a destra*. The reason why such logical conditions as these do not prevail here is due to the fact that the country is ruled not by any democratic party but by the Establishment.

The Establishment, briefly, is the English constitution, and the group of institutions and outlying agencies built round it to assist in its protection; it naturally also includes all those who stand like commissionaires before these protective institutions to protect *them*. The word derives, of course, from the ecclesiastical establishment of the Anglican church, which is a political scheme to harness the religious instincts of middle class loyalty to the state. No church in the world has ever had so vague and general a theology: it can, without self-contradiction, support almost any change of constitution, government or policy—providing that it does possess one such to support at any given time. All English vicars, in short, are Vicars of Bray; and certainly all bishops' wives are Mrs. Proudies, pillars of the constitution a thousand times more than they are of any theological point of view.

In the nineteenth century the Church (not considered here because it is no more than the senior common room of that greater Establishment institution, the public school) underwent a final development, associating it with the constitutional changes of that time. Now a knowledge of the character of English society in the middle of the nineteenth century is fundamental to an understanding of the development of the Establishment, and of its true consistency in the middle of the twentieth century; and therefore of the ruling motives of the government of Britain at the present time also. For all countries are deeply and permanently marked by the character of the epoch when they become (if they ever do so) the greatest on earth. The ambition of national groups to become not just great nations but the greatest is described by Shatov in Dostoievsky's *The Possessed*: '*a truly great people can never reconcile itself to playing second-fiddle in the affairs of humanity, not even to playing an important part, but always and exclusively the chief part*'. Speaking nearly a hundred years before Russia had come within sight of the fulfilment of this aspiration, Shatov could not realize that, once fulfilment of this kind is indeed achieved by a nation, that nation inevitably rests on its laurels, the very institutions which it had built to realize its greatness tending to slow down future development and resist innovation; what happens in the case of all such once greatest nations, Britain included, is seen most vividly in the case of Spain, where for four hundred years any idea, mood or political aspiration which had not existed in the golden sixteenth century has been automatically frowned upon as 'Un-Spanish'. Now Britain was the greatest nation in the world between 1830 and 1870—from the end of the period of political adjustment following the Napoleonic Wars until the rise of German and American industrial power. Although Bismarck detected weakness in Britain as early as 1864—at the time of the Schleswig crisis—the world's assumption was that Britain remained the greatest world power until 1914—though, for this argument, there is no economic substantiation. However, in general terms, it is enough to repeat the platitude that Victorian England was the greatest national group on earth—without worrying too much when precisely this period began or ended.

Now it is this Victorian England, with all its prejudices, ignorances and inhibitions, that the Establishment sets out to defend. The Establishment is the present-day institutional museum of Britain's past greatness. Consider first *the Public Schools*, which are analysed in this symposium by Mr. John Vaizey. The whole slant of the public school education—as Mr. Vaizey shows—is to provide a continuous stream of socially gifted and athletic amateurs to act as proconsuls in, however, an Empire that no longer exists in 1959. The atmosphere, the ideals, the knowledge inculcated in the public schools is totally anachronistic; but each year a new phalanx of recruits for the Establishment is produced; and one uses the word 'phalanx' advisedly, for it recalls the military unit with which the Macedonians succeeded in overwhelming the Athenian democracy in the fourth century B.C.; and already today the assimilation of these redundant pro-consuls is causing social disruption—an ever-increasing stratification of society and the increasing dissemination of political points of view in 1959 more proportionally *ultra* than existed in 1859. Then there is the *Army*: in the nineteenth century this force had a certain limited task to perform—the policing of the world Pax Britannica; as Mr. Raven shows in his essay, Britain has never needed an army to make wars, an officer corps with its own professional ambitions such as the Germans persuaded themselves they required to unite the country; Britain has simply needed a group of amateur gentlemen who could be superior without difficulty and without too much offence in various parts of the world. In 1959 the role of the British Army, with no Pax Britannica to police, is to act as a standing temptation to successive governments to use force to make up for, and to worsen, the mistakes of colonial policy. The past role of the army has also lured successive governments into supposing that, because Britain was once the greatest power, she must still aspire to the trappings, if not the facts, of continuing greatness; hence, alongside the maintenance of a redundant standing army, Britain has built up a stockpile of redundant atom and hydrogen bombs. The contemporary 'defence' policy of both Russia and America do possess their own brutal logic; that of Britain does not; every year, about the time of the first crocus, the British government prints a military document usually known as the Defence White Paper; its illogicalities are invariably so obvious that the minister responsible for it, the Minister of Defence, has given up pretending that it makes sense; the nation as a whole, however, soothed by the grave apocalyptic tones in which defence policy is always discussed, knowing those tones to be sagacious-sounding Establishment tones, generously supposes that the lack of logic must really be on their own part, and that the real sense is carefully hidden, like an atom secret, in some tin box in the War Office. If the nation's gullibility is easily understandable, and if the ordinary man can be excused if he turns away from the Defence White Paper, and other documents in the same series, to refresh his eyes with a television quiz-game or his ears with a strident band-show on the wireless, what, one might demand, of the politicians? Surely they are not so easily deluded.

Alas! Mr. Hollis in his essay on 'Parliament and the Establishment' paints a gloomy picture. The real source of political tension in Britain today may be the continuing struggle between capital and labour. But neither of the two political parties reflects this antagonism. They may be financed entirely by the two sides in the industrial dispute; but the parties have to work an old parliamentary system, perfected in the nineteenth century upon eighteenth and seventeenth century foundations. In consequence, both parties are led to adopt as their leaders men who, though untypical of the industrial struggle and of the greater part of their own followers, are nevertheless capable of manipulating the debating chamber technique of government evolved in the nine-teenth century (it is of course a mistake to think that the corrupt parliamentary practice of the eighteenth century had anything in common with the system which developed, admittedly gradually at first, after 1832). Take the two last leaders of both political parties: Sir Anthony Eden and Mr. Macmillan would have been quite at home in the House of Commons at any time since the Reform Bill; and so would, rather more surprisingly in the party of change, Earl Attlee and Mr. Gaitskell. As for earlier Labour leaders, Mr. Lansbury—a true son of his party—was not a success; while it is difficult to think of any epoch in any country since the Renaissance where the peculiar talents of Mr. Ramsay Macdonald could not have been successfully exploited. There is, therefore, in both political parties a common acceptance of certain rules, which often prevent the airing of honest views in parliament; and these rules are simply the rules of debate evolved a hundred years ago.

There is Dr. Balogh's essay on the Civil Service and Mr. Sandelson's essay on the City: both are institutions whose organization and *raison d'être* derive directly from the needs of Victorian England: their shibboleths, professional traditions, and aspirations are in every case exactly one hundred years old. Both were developed in order to make smooth the functioning of the old liberal freedoms, to break away feudal or ecclesiastical fetters on the search for prosperity. They are institutions essentially pre-, as well as anti-, collectivist in outlook, since

B

they were developed at a time when it was still a revolutionary step to build a factory and when the real enemy was still the remains of feudalism. But at the present time both are hindrances to the realization of a true socially-conscious society; the City, Mr. Sandelson demonstrates, is the heart of economic conservatism—the very ideas which in the nineteenth century were the driving force of expansion, being now a brake on the best development of the national effort.

Reading through these enquiring essays, the reader will gain the impression that he is looking at an aerial photograph of one of those great, usually southern, cities, where a number of handsome classical buildings—housing the central bank, the ministry of war, the telephone exchange—surround a huge but totally deserted square: emptiness of the square indicates the emptiness of the anachronistic frame of mind which the Establishment inculcates in all spheres, including others than those purely governmental; all the points of view were of course laid down in the nineteenth century: in painting, for instance, there are certain great masters, all Italians, for Rembrandt is too difficult and Velazquez too profound, to compare with the obvious beauties of Raphael, Titian and Veronese. An Establishment point of view in painting undoubtedly, to an unbelievable extent, reflects midnineteenth century canons of judgement; there are still circles in England for whom an appreciation of the Impressionists is an esoteric taste and for whom El Greco is still 'insane'. The same prejudices are to be found throughout the field of art and Britain in 1959 undoubtedly has the reputation of being the one nation in the world where it is possible to hear Wagner solemnly denounced as a revolutionary. In literature, Proust heads a long list of writers whom the even comparatively literate elsewhere have absorbed long ago but for whom the Establishment has no time. Let it not be thought I am criticizing the *intelligence* of the Establishment; I am merely pointing out that in other countries the far fewer number of people who have comparable intelligences to the British establishmentarians are far more intellectually or aesthetically alive. Morally, for instance, in England the whole intellectual revolution caused by Marx and Freud, the development of a frame of mind which is prepared to admit that all behaviour, 'good' and 'bad', is classifiable in the same continuum, is ignored by the Establishment; so is the closely connected philosophical revolution

associated originally with the name of Wittgenstein; in place
of these things there is a habit of categorizing good and bad
not in relation to religion or to any revealed truth, but simply
according as whether it is approved or disapproved by Establishment canons—which means, more or less, is it 'done'—which
itself means: was it done or not done a hundred years ago? A
similar atavism is seen in the sphere of private moral behaviour:
the 'immorality' of 1859 (which allowed to males a great deal more
freedom than to females) is socially acceptable; anything more
blatant, more modern, is not permissible.

Now the great buildings round the empty square are not the
only buildings in the Establishment, nor are such buildings its only
powerful manifestations: from the late nineteenth century onwards,
for example, there has been developed a magnificent line of
Establishment thoroughbreds, almost buildings in themselves,
who have exerted an unusual influence on the politics of the
country. We see Dr. Jowett preparing his undergraduates for this
particular rôle—and watching his policy succeed, as Milner,
Curzon and the rest advance majestically from office to office, and
emolument to emolument. Now these men—and their last, and
most baneful, flowering was the group of publicists and rich men
gathered under the elm trees of Cliveden in the late 'thirties—
were politically very able, but they possessed absolutely no real
political views at all. They enjoyed, even worshipped, power, but
the idea that the purpose of political power is consciously to seek
to make the world a better place never occurred to them—Curzon,
for instance, was a Knight of the Garter, a marquess, and the
second most important man of the kingdom before he realized
that the working classes had the same coloured skin as himself.
Yet he was a man who had spent his whole life in politics—the
most gregarious profession in the world. And these men, and their
in most cases less formidable successors alive today, have built up
around themselves a whole churchful of Establishment rites and
holy days and holy places: Empire Day and Christmas Day
(because of the monarch's broadcast) are the chief Establishment
feasts; and there are saints too—St. Alexander Cadogan, St.
Kenneth Clark, St. Kindersley, St. Edward Bridges; these are
needed to carry out heraldic functions at such occasions as the
Royal Academy Banquet, the Trooping of the Colour, or the
Lord Mayor's Show and to staff new Establishment buildings,

such as the B.B.C. This new building of the Establishment (how reminiscent it is of all those other new buildings in Oxford or Cambridge, colleges which were built at the same time in the 'twenties) is examined by Mr. Henry Fairlie in the last essay of this book: it was Mr. Fairlie who first publicized the use of the word Establishment in his weekly articles in the *Spectator*, and it is fitting that he should have the last word on the subject here.

(The word 'Establishment' simply indicates the assumption of the attributes of a state church by certain powerful institutions and people; in general these may be supposed to be effectively beyond democratic control. Various contributors, Mr. Hollis in particular, interpret the word in a slightly different way, but the definition which I have given is generally accepted by them all. Mr. Fairlie first used the word in print during the Burgess and Maclean revelations in September 1955; he alleged that the two diplomats had been 'protected' by the Establishment. The word was, however, in use among the thoughtful at least a year previously; I recall myself employing it while passing the Royal Academy in a taxi in company with Mr. Paul Johnson of the *New Statesman* in August 1954. In 1953, however, the word was not in use at all. It is probable that the introduction of the word indicated a certain increase in looking at English politics in a French style; those who detect an 'Establishment' at work in England are the cousins of those who in France have detected the more obvious role of 'the 400 families'.)

To those who desire to see the resources and talents of Britain fully developed and extended, there is no doubt that the fusty Establishment, with its Victorian views and standards of judgement, must be destroyed; the authors of the following essays make their own suggestions as to how (as well as why) this should be done; the editor, however, cannot refrain from pointing out that it is in childhood that the men who make the present Establishment are trained; and that therefore we shall not be free of the Establishment frame of mind, permeating all aspects of life and society, and constantly re-appearing even when apparently uprooted, until the public schools are completely swept away, at whatever cost to the temporary peace of the country. First in importance the subject is thus first in this book in order of appearance.

The Public Schools

by *John Vaizey*

Age 29. Economist. Formerly Fellow of St. Catherine's College, Cambridge, now teaching at Oxford. Author of *The Costs of Education, Guinness's Brewery in the Irish Economy* (with Patrick Lynch), *Scenes from Institutional Life*, and other books.

INTELLIGENT discussion of the public schools is handicapped by the fact that they are indescribably funny. I am forced to this conclusion by reading attempts to describe them: take this, for example, from George Orwell—the best critic there has been. He sums up the quintessence of what we find funny:

'You are at Greyfriars, a rosy-cheeked boy of fourteen in posh tailor-made clothes, sitting down to tea in your study in the Remove passage after an exciting game of football which was won by an odd goal in the last half-minute. There is a cosy fire in the study, and outside the wind is whistling. The King is on his throne and the pound is worth a pound. . . . Mauleverer has just got another fiver and we are all settling down to a tremendous tea of sausages, sardines, crumpets, potted meat, jam and doughnuts. After tea we shall sit round the study fire having a good laugh at Billy Bunter and discussing the team for next week's match against Rookwood. Everything is safe, solid and unquestionable. Everything will be the same for ever and ever.'

This comes from his essay on boys' magazines; it is, of course, a parody but it is alarming how nature imitates art. If we turn, for example, to Anthony Powell we find the same scene in its essentials.

The public schools lend themselves to humour; they are the source of irony on the theme of social-climbing (dear to the hearts of the class-ridden English) as well as pomposity, conceit, homosexuality, religion and philistinism. It would be a pity, however, if a discussion of their place in our society were to be side-tracked by a succession of jokes; though they are in themselves extremely amusing, their public role is too serious to be neglected.

By public schools we mean only a proportion of the private schools that cater for about one-eleventh of English children. In Scotland, Wales and Northern Ireland most people go to schools

23

run by (or administered for) the state; in England, mainly because of the meanness of the local authorities, it has been a tradition among the better-off that they should pay for their children's education. Many such schools are decayed chocolate-painted Victorian villas with girls learning to type in the upstairs front bedroom while tiny tots do elocution in the larder, all under the instruction of underpaid and untrained ladies *d'un certain age* and uncertain social position. Within this sector of the fee-paying education, however, is a hard core of fairly respectable schools that have come to be called 'public schools', originally because some of them were reorganized in the mid-nineteenth century of public authority; then by contagion as their headmasters joined the headmasters' conference; then, by aspiration, among the rest. Tutors are familiar with boys from remote and (to judge from their products) dismally disheartening schools whose one parrot-cry is 'It's a public school, you know': often, this is almost all they can say, even in Latin. At one time three boys in succession from a school called 'The Wrekin School' said this to a colleague of mine: they stopped when he enquired whether they were known as 'old wrecks'. There is, then, no union of public schools; there is, rather, a hard core of twenty or so schools of recognized status, and a following of perhaps a hundred others which aspire to this status and are, increasingly, attaining it.

Their status is a social one. It is not associated necessarily with boarding education, though it often is, but there are some public schools, St. Paul's and the City of London, for instance, which deal with day boys. One chain of public schools is administered by the Girls Public Day School Trust. Nevertheless a high proportion of public schools are boarding schools.

Their status does not spring essentially from their fee-paying character. Many of them are charitable foundations and provide entry by scholarship, while others are in receipt of grants from the state and are under the obligation, as 'direct-grant' schools, to provide a proportion of their places for children sent by local authorities. Nevertheless, the element of fee-paying is substantial, especially in boarding schools, and may be considered a common characteristic.

Above all, the schools are 'independent' of local authorities, and are exceptionally socially selective. These characteristics —boarding education, fee-paying, freedom from local control and social selection—combine to produce the instantly-recognizable public school; any diminution in one or more of these four characteristics suggests that the school is a marginal case. But there is one more element: an emphasis on the teaching of Dr. Arnold, frequent mention of the words 'character', 'leadership', 'English', 'tradition'—which is extraordinarily important. The more marginal a school, the more its products emphasize this sort of stuff: as the Duke of Clarence says in Mr. Hugh Thomas's novel *The Oxygen Age*—'. . . leadership therefore remains an attribute we shall continue to prize . . . character is indeed leadership . . . leadership is character . . . wahhahaha.' For the last mumbled word 'tradition' is a possible substitute. In my experience boys from a marginal school (Durham) believe that their O.T.C. was formed by the Venerable Bede and that St. Cuthbert was the first (and best) Captain of Rugger.

They seem to be taught that they are society's natural leaders; it is consciously instilled at the worst schools and (more insidiously) assumed at the best. And this teaching is effective because it is true: they do throw up the leaders in most important spheres. In 1955 over half the entrants to Oxford and Cambridge came from public schools; in 1958, the Grigg committee on the armed services regretted that so few officers came from schools other than these; all the High Court Judges but one; all the Bishops but one; almost all Tory M.P.s and a third of the Labour M.P.s; the whole Cabinet—the list could go on. Of course, as the Colonel says to two eighteen-year-olds in my favourite book *Tell England*, by Ernest Raymond: 'Eighteen years ago you were born for this day (4th August, 1914). Through the last eighteen years you've been educated for it. Your birth and breeding were given you that you might officer England's youth in this hour.'

They are officered still, forty years after the hour, by the same 'birth and breeding'.

But, also they lead in the Opposition. As the lovely sinuous youth Doe says in *Tell England*: 'I think I'm a Socialist. . . . They may be visionary, but they are idealists. And I think it's up to us public schoolboys to lead the great mass of uneducated people, who can't articulate their needs. I'd love to be their leader;' and, by God, they are, too. Move over Keir Hardie, Crossman is here.

The public schools rest upon a firm economic foundation. Mr. Lydall points out in *British Incomes and Savings* that in 1953 over 90 per cent of those with incomes over £1,000 a year were paying fees for their children's education. This class is growing enormously rapidly; the public schools are full to overflowing and have queues of entrants. Endowment rains upon them; industry has just given them £3½ millions to pay for science laboratories: they are subsidized by the state which exempts their endowments from tax and allows companies to pay school-fees—it even pays some fees itself in order to get 'officer-material' for its own rather bad public school, Welbeck Abbey. All the signs suggest that this royal road to the good jobs is getting wider and paved with more and more gold. According to Roy Lewis it is ten times easier to be successful in business if you are a public school boy: fathers in business take the hint.

The public schools are less open to attack now than they have ever been, despite the fact that they stick out like a sore thumb in an otherwise democratic society—or a society that at least likes to pretend it is democratic. Thirty years ago their literate products obviously loathed them—books from *The Loom of Youth* on savaged them and in 1934 (as Philip Toynbee tells it) Esmond Romilly at the age of fifteen founded a magazine called *Out of Bounds* which was 'against Reaction, Militarism and Fascism in the Public Schools'. 'This was a period,' writes Toynbee, 'of noble schoolboy passion, when the Officers' Training Corps, fagging and corporal punishment were ogres, more or less freshly discovered.' Such a thing is impossible now.

There are a number of reasons for this. The middle class believes itself to be poor and downtrodden, paying for a welfare-state that others enjoy. In 1958, in a public opinion sample in Cambridge nearly 80 per cent of undergraduates from public schools called themselves Tories while only rather more than 10 per cent called themselves Socialists. Most of them believed in God. In other words, they conformed.

Then, life at public schools is believed to be hard and tough compared with the pampered life led at L.C.C. Comprehensives: as one matron wrote to the *Sunday Times*:

'One good thing I can say for fagging: the public school boy takes National Service in his stride. The lad from a working-class home, whose mother has not only cleaned his shoes, but tied his tie and fastened his shoe-laces up to school-leaving age, is loudly indignant when confronted with the menial tasks of Service life.'

The influence of twenty years of National Service has led people to believe that they should train themselves for a life where 'fagging', corporal punishment, discipline, etc., are more appropriate than the values of a democratic society. Above all, the children are conscious that their parents have often 'slaved' or 'starved themselves' (both of them terms frequently used with very little actual but a great deal of psychological truth) in order to buy their children the 'best' education. The young of this generation admire their parents and are guiltily grateful to them.

Above all, it is true *in some senses* that the education is the best! Although we are often told that Eton, Harrow, Winchester (the example varies with the most recent Young Conservative outing) are so uncomfortable that nobody from the working classes would voluntarily go to them, there is a good deal of exaggeration in this. They all have playing fields, and quantities of halls, rooms, gymnasia, laboratories, libraries and dining halls on a scale almost unknown to other schools. Further, they have very big staffs (the pupil-teacher ratio is probably one-third the national average) and the staffs are—in the better schools—often highly qualified. The worship of games has been reduced and, after all, most children like playing games, so that they welcome the chance to play a great variety of games with skilled and intelligent coaching. There is plenty of music, jazz-clubs as well as 'cellos and pianos and Bach oratorios; there is drama; there is art. Less and less of the instruction is mechanical rote-learning of dead languages: the bright boys do physics and chemistry and the dull boys do economics (I examine them). One thinks of friends teaching at these schools and envies their pupils: one man is a highly-skilled rugger player who is capable of dealing with rugger as an exercise in applied intelligence; he is also a good zoologist excited by his subject; he is a good man who worries about his sensitive pupils —and there are hosts of delightful people like him.

Their lives are hard. They seem to work more than some other teachers, and they are rarely paid much more than Burnham scale; they are often shut up in the country and life away from the school seems a long way away. But they have small classes; they are conscious that they are at 'the top' and their life has that ordered dignity amid charming surroundings that appeals to many people in many walks of life—the universities, the army, the navy, and the church, for example. Above all, they feel that their work is achieving its purpose.

What is its purpose? They provide, for payment, the goods that parents pay for. Essentially, their feeling is that of satisfied *entrepreneurs* who know they can deliver their very high quality goods. In contrast with teachers in Borstals, for example, they are encouraging their children to follow their parents' example and accept their philosophy. They encourage the boys to work hard and seriously and they measure their achievements fairly ruthlessly, by the test of the G.C.E. results and entrance to Oxford, Cambridge, Sandhurst and the medical schools. On top of this, they take games incredibly seriously; they want their boys to be fit and tough. Because of this they serve meals that are well-balanced, they insist on adequate sleep; personal hygiene is important—it all goes in the concept of 'training', and (consciously) the game that is being trained for is seen as a paradigm of life itself where these qualities will be useful.

Both these purposes, the training of the mind and the toughening of the body (underlaid as they are by fervent support from parents), are successfully achieved. Moreover, in themselves they are obviously of the highest importance and are clearly more 'right' than 'wrong'. Of course they are capable of distortion: a young man can be seen *entirely* as a budding scientist (it seems a shame for the argument that so many should be German Jews) or *entirely* as a perfectly working games-player: but working-class boys are even more prone to this distortion, by working too hard for their career, or making a career of their sport.

On top of these two eminently sensible objectives, however, come others that are more suspicious. The learning and the getting-fit are represented as a part of the 'training for leadership' which many public-schoolmasters see as their social role. In fact, as I have said, it is a role that they play to perfection. It happens to be a very wrong role. It infects the whole set-up with a certain smugness and a certain frightening *élite* concept. The word 'breeding' is often on their lips, despite genetic studies that show leadership to be a social trait, and social studies that show many of the middle-class to be *arrivistes* in every sense of the word. Many of these boys go around looking for people to lead: they

actually say at the university interviews that they feel they have
been trained to lead; this despite the fact that in our democracy
we are all supposed (in one situation or another) to be leaders *and*
led, and that these boys are utterly ignorant of the lives of over
95 per cent of their fellow-countrymen.

This leadership mystique is allied to the consciously Platonic
part played by the children's segregation from their families and
neighbours in both the public boarding and day schools. At first
sight—say to a visiting Martian—it is incredible that a Western
community should send its children away from the age of eight
to eighteen to a kind of monastery or nunnery. Why do they do it?

Clearly because like must be taught with like. All arguments
about boarding education boil down to the fact that the top people
tend to be geographically scattered and they like to herd their
children together—more especially, they like to herd the boys
together. Even in day schools the children are expected to travel
a considerable distance to school, and school takes up by far the
greater part of their day. The schools are given a major place in
a child's life, greater even sometimes than his family, greater
certainly than that of his own home environment. This pressure
for institutionalizing children is violently in contrast with the
trends in the rest of social life: psychologists, educationalists,
doctors, social workers, penologists, geriatricians all argue that a
human being is de-humanized by institutional life. Yet more and
more people wish to send their children to institutions, usually
for one sex only, for ten years of their lives. Is what is true for the
deprived child, the sick child, the mad child not true for the rich
child?

What takes place in such a school is, first, a rigorous intellectual
and athletic training programme: intellect is pursued to an extreme,
perhaps at Winchester and Manchester Grammar School,
physique at places like Haileybury and Felsted. Above all, however, there is a tremendous amount of social adjustment to their
own peer-group—boys of roughly the same age, or girls of
roughly the same age. They are given common standards of
speech, dress and manners and these standards are imposed by a
complex social system of mutual adjustment in which the boys in
one year learn from those in that just above it. Hence the importance of fagging and the prefect system.

To a foreign educationalist it is astonishing that such power should be given to an eighteen-year-old as is given to a prefect: what makes it work is the restricted set of social values which are allowed to operate in the situation, and the acceptance by both the prefect and the fag that these values are there to be acquired.

What are the values? Independence is said to be one. I find it hard to believe. A fag at Repton is having his own meals, shelter and social environment provided, and is treated as a 'little' boy at an age when the majority of boys are already working in factories, offices, shops and farms for forty-four hours a week, when they are taking girls to dances and are smoking, and are contributing to the upkeep of their home. They are, too, usually helping to keep the home clean, despite tales to the contrary.

Self-discipline is another. I find it hard to believe that discipline so seriously enforced is at all linked to the genuine self-discipline that a wide range of social choice requires. Blinkers are being, perhaps permanently, given them.

How to live with people? This manifestly does not apply to girls, babies, the sick, old people, the working classes, negroes . . . it can only apply in a very restricted sense of how to get on with boys of roughly the same age from similar income groups which is by no means the same thing. How many of them could cope with life, day in day out, in a three-bedroomed council flat, or in a back-to-back in Leeds? This is not necessarily a criticism of them or the system that produces them: it is merely stating the fact that all is not what it seems to be at first sight.

Patriotism, or something like it?—after all they are going to be public servants, sitting on committees and in the House. But listen to this:

'B—.   J—, like so many, is debating whether to work in England or overseas. Farming is his job. A big question. Talking of work in general many fear that another Socialist Government would reduce the country to a position of comparative helplessness among the nations and that the outlook for a man with initiative would be bleak indeed. Of course the unscrupulous bloke will make a living, but we do not train chaps for that. Canada has a vast potential and the Rhodesias and East Africa, with the Dominions down under, all offer scope. Capital is nearly always the stumbling block. The roots of the middle-aged are probably too deep in this country for emigration, but the young chaps have the chance to escape what so many fear is the inglorious and sordid future of a country that allows shop-stewards the license they are permitted today. I will not advise, in any case generalization is useless. Overseas our chaps must maintain the standards they learnt here.'

This seditious tripe (unredeemed by a note: 'A.A.N.T— has M.B.E. So glad.') was issued by a public school house-master to his Old Boys on the first Sunday after the Anglo-French pilots left the Suez Canal (a day named by Hugh Thomas for St. Selwyn). It is not untypical of what many such men have said and are saying. Whatever it is, it is not patriotism, nor even loyalty. It is the philosophy of *sauve qui peut*, applied to classes rather than to individuals: it is the antithesis of sensible training to be an Englishman now, today; to be an Englishman who understands his fellow-countrymen and his country; where, indeed, the children of shop-stewards outnumber public school boys. Even in the Rhodesias there are more blacks than old school ties.

Religion? Ostensibly all public schools put great emphasis on religion; most of them are Church of England and are fairly evangelical in tone (perhaps that is why there seems so much of the eternal schoolboy in the hearty evangelical), but some are Roman Catholic, Methodist and even Quaker, while Clifton has a Jewish House. (So far as I can discover there are no schools for Muslims though a few exist for Humanists.) Indeed judging from the public opinion poll of Cambridge undergraduates, the regular routine of chapel and religious teaching, reinforced by S.C.M. camps, school societies and the rite of confirmation, tends to persist at least into later life, and one has the impression that Anglicanism is itself rather a public school thing. All the Bishops think so: when they talk about 'our schools' they usually mean not the insanitary slums that agricultural labourers' children go to, but Repton, etc. There is even a school near Leatherhead catering almost exclusively for the sons of Anglican parsons.

In a social sense, then, religion does seem to have rather a key role. It does not, however, seem to have any great ethical bias: public school boys are not notorious for taking all that they have and giving it to the poor nor, so far as can be seen, are they noticeably backward in fornication, adultery and homosexuality. (They are backward in incest, probably because they see so little of their families.) Of course many might think that the religious bias of the school life would be a good thing if there were any truth in religion: this is a fundamental objection and is regarded as rather below the belt.

Pursuing values in the abstract I seem rapidly to be getting to an impasse. Let us argue the thing back, from people. What are public school boys like? I speak of them at Oxford and Cambridge. An observant pupil tells me that "physically, they seem to be bigger than the rest of us with especially long legs. Their faces tend to be long and lean, or fleshy; in every case they seem to be permanently twenty-five years of age. Their hair is longish, and either very fair and straight or dark and curly; their lips are slightly bulging; their voices loud and confident or soft and penetrating. They are always very well shaven; never blue-jowled or side-boarded; they tend to look very clean and to smell of Imperial Leather soap and bay rum. Their clothes do not include zip-fronted knitted garments, gaberdine raincoats, bright blue or brown suits with stripes, brown shoes with toecaps, Y-fronts, suspenders, tie-pins, lapel-badges, or leopard skin bathing trunks; they never use Brylcreem, or bicycles with low handle-bars; they hold cigarettes between the index finger and the second finger and can smoke pipes without over-much affectation; they can wear hats, overcoats with raglan sleeves; or British warms bought outside the Charing Cross Road, old loose jackets with leather elbows, corded or very dark grey trousers, big brown brogues, simple and very old suede shoes, light ankle-boots, clerical grey suits with a coloured striped shirt and a very prominent white collar, braces, institutional ties (usually a bum cricket team—'The Cammels'), or Paisley ties, dressing gowns which are too short because they have had them at school, an abundance of rather ragged and slightly grey underwear. Their clothes are covered in Cash's labels (especially on the parts of socks you can see) and their handkerchiefs are numbered (their mothers do not wash them).

"Sport deserves special mention. No public school boy is ashamed of nudity; grammar school boys shy away in changing-rooms from these towel-draped steaming bodies; at odd hours the public school boy goes for a trot (a five-mile bash through the Oxford streets in very long shorts and a sweater with a towel round his neck) and plays squash for relaxation after dinner; as I walk through Oxford across the Giler, down Parks Road and along the Turl I see figures that would be greeted in Lewisham or Birkenhead with shrieks of derision. Above all, the public school boy has a plethora of old equipment—bats, rackets, rugger boots, jock-straps, boxes, lacrosse sticks, fives gloves and old ice-skates—all the equipment of the lesser-known sports.

"Public school boys are bloody rude unless they make a decision to be charming. They are deferent but somehow equal in dealing with older people—they call anyone over twenty-eight 'Sir' but they talk about the same things: house-masters, winter sports and common acquaintance, etc. (as Lord Attlee always says). With the lower orders they have a 'my man' attitude—frequent use of 'please' and 'thank you', with an expectation of instant compliance with their wishes, all overlaid with an air of consideration—'how's the wife'—that is the equivalent of finding comfortable lodgings for their men while sleeping under the lorry in their great coats (as Michael, the perverted leader, does in Iris Murdoch's *The Bell*). They tend to eat like pigs; it is those poised on social brinks who worry about table manners. Public school boys steal and break other people's possessions and it is wrong to complain.

"They do not talk like Nancy Mitford. In contrast with the working classes their speech is coherent, but rather light. They are very confident and emotionally quite uninvolved in what they say; they must never be in a position where it is possible to be snubbed, ridiculed or ruffled. They must talk deprecatingly about their own, their family's and their friends' achievements, yet they are intensely ambitious and ruthlessly efficient in achieving serious objectives. They rarely see their parents and they tend to treat them as they treat other older people; above all, they have not rejected their parents' values, and have a cash-nexus with them which is quite unknown to the grammar school scholar."

How about the public school girl? My pupil goes on: "She is open-air and has a pale oval face, and full lips, with dark straight hair; she is slightly short and has very mobile calves; she tends to wear headscarves with fox's masks on them, and riding macs. or fur-lined three-quarter length jackets. When dressed up she wears black jersey-frocks, strings of pearls, and pale pastel-coloured jumpers under suits. Her shoes are usually very flat or exceptionally high. Her finger-nails are very sensible and covered in uncoloured varnish. Altogether she is attractive in an antiseptic and practical kind of way.

"She assumes that every man they meet (working-class girls

call them boys) has been at a public school, an officer in a good regiment and—usually—at Oxford or Cambridge; any other man, by definition, works in a factory and is capable of a Luddite outrage fraught with sexual significance. They all live in the country, which they love, and imagine that everyone has permanently kept one gelding and several bitches. (One is reminded of the *Daily Sketch* photograph of Princess Anne embracing a pony, with the caption 'Just like Mummy'.) They marry very young, but not like working-class girls, boys who are roughly the same age; they marry men at least eight or ten years older than themselves. They have then several children rapidly. (This is closely connected with their expectation of an income adequate to keep up the ponies, etc.)''

What do public school boys read? "On their shelves are unread leather-bound volumes, and sometimes Somerset Maugham, Nancy Mitford, the Churchill war histories, and some popular biographies. Not much good writing on the whole: most of Dr. Leavis's followers seem to be grammar school boys; Lord David Cecil is more in the public school boy's line of country. Their intellectual interests tend to be fairly highly vocational—the bar, the church, schoolmastering or 'leading' (hence the biographies). On the whole, they do not read.''

From this picture a certain amount can be deduced. They are above all a minority group; what sociologists call a sub-culture. They have a pronounced and highly idiosyncratic pattern of life which tends to differ markedly from that of other parts of the society in which their sub-culture exists. Partly this difference is explicable in economic terms; they have more money and so live in bigger houses, can travel abroad, afford cars and can have servants of a sort. But this is by no means all, or even a major part of the explanation. Some working-class boys are as expensively dressed as public school boys; they are often more expensively barbered; sometimes they are cleaner. No, it is partly a matter of developing an attitude; the attitude, in fact, of the Top People. It is mainly, it seems, at school that this is acquired.

What, in other words, do they seem to believe about life itself?

They are withdrawn and disinclined for serious discussion that involves personal involvement or commitment. This gives their conversation a lightness, or a lack of passion, that accords closely with their diffident, somewhat distant manner. In part, this is connected with a very well-developed sense of superiority. This is in striking contrast with working-class life, where passions are easily aroused and where commitment of some kind—even to a football team—is a customary thing. The minority value of being uncommitted accords well with a number of civilized values; it is dangerous because it is allied to a condescension not only to the majority but to the things that matter in life itself. Art, conversation—it is an easy jump from this to a quiet connoisseurship in ideas, where nothing really matters any more. 'But it is, if possible, still more difficult to think, or try to think, really honestly about your life and other people's lives. And the trouble is that thinking about these things is *not thrilling*, but often downright nasty. Being timid I don't like clashes and particularly not with people I like. But I'd rather have a clash than mere superficial talk.' Here Wittgenstein expresses the opposite of a public school value.

Lawrence is the exponent of another value which is the opposite of public school values: 'So, we know the first great purpose of Democracy: that each man shall be spontaneously himself—'; he is the exponent of the opposition because, as we have seen, the products of the public schools are remarkably brain-washed and they are the opposite of spontaneous.

With rare percipience Raymond Williams sees that in the public school culture the notion of hierarchy is deeply embedded and that this notion is deeply disguised by calling it 'service'. They are trained to lead, quite consciously, but the leadership is ennobled by linking it to a romantic conception of 'service'. 'A very large part of English middle-class education is devoted to the training of servants. This is much more its characteristic than a training for leadership, as the stress on conformity and in respect for authority shows. In so far it is, by definition, the training of upper servants, it includes, of course, the instilling of that kind of confidence which will enable the upper servants to supervise and direct the lower servants. Order must be maintained there, by good management, and in this respect the function is not service but government. Yet the upper servant is not to think of his own interests. He must subordinate these to a larger good, which is called the Queen's peace, or national security, or law and order, or the public weal.'

Williams has here got hold of the heart of the matter. The public schools train people to accept the cultural norms which they exist to perpetuate and they do this as ruthlessly as any cell in Peking. As a result, while numbers of people walk about convinced that they are wearing themselves to the bone for the public good, they are really walking about keeping the Establishment going.

(I mean, if they are wearing themselves out for us, who asked them to? Not me, or you. Them. In fact, of course, most of them wear themselves out for themselves.)

The notion of 'service' is a 'tradition'. Now tradition is a word frequently employed in this context and I am anxious to examine it carefully.

Most 'tradition' in the sense of doing what has been done for many generations is as bogus as the coronation service or Buckingham Palace: they are Victorian or Edwardian inventions at the earliest. Old school ties only date from the turn of the century. An interesting example of this is a tradition concerning dress or games that has been invented within living memory, or a house that has recently been founded, or a modern school like Stowe. On the other hand the public schools have very effectively captured English history by incorporating it in their 'tradition'; in a very important sense they try to capture the main themes and make the rest of society out-casts. The throne, the law, the army and navy (not the R.A.F.), the empire, the church, the older universities and the constitution have been interpreted as of their very own construction; they identify with them (to use a psychological term); they resent criticism of them—in other words, they have pinched them.

This, I take it, is one of the major objections to the public school system; it lies at the root of the Establishment; and in so doing it deeply divides the national culture and makes the activities of other people second-rate compared with the Establishment activities, according to the public system of values imposed by their own powerful institutions. In a very important sense they are institution-worshippers. They deny the validity of working-class cultural activities—soccer, collective action (the activities of shop-stewards are always criticized), and so on; as a result on the whole the other ranks tend to lose their activities to the predatory demands of the officers' mess.

Life thus imitates the public school. The institution claims all and takes all; it teaches them to appropriate and they do.

Every system, however, has its deviants, the people it rejects and who reject it. The trouble is that their rejection is on the terms of the public schools: it is the antithesis of the thesis stated by the system, so they are always *involved*; their life is a perpetual running away from school and waiting to be fetched back, as Denton Welch found when he ran away from Repton and Toynbee when he ran away from Rugby. This is what gives the Labour Party its particular flavour; in no sense can it *disregard* the values implicit in the public school system; it can only deny or affirm them, because its leaders are all (through their own origins, or their sons) having a love affair with some posh school.

One major objection to public schools is that by herding young people of one sex together they prevent in some cases the development of normal sexual relations. Freud has a word for this! In fact this is a special aspect of a general case; the public school system is to be condemned not only because it retards hetero-sexuality but because it distorts so strongly the free development of the boys and girls who are put through it. No competent foreign educationalist could possibly support the imposition of values and *mores* in the way that is here undertaken; nor the full-time pre-occupation of the children with school and its affairs; nor the separation of society into two such distinct cultures.

It is important to realize that the public schools are not wholly to be admired as educational institutions. Their teachers are rarely trained, and at some the teaching is, by all accounts, dreadful; especially for the academically weaker streams. Certainly there seems little effort in a number of schools to devise an appropriate syllabus for them. It is only recently, too, that many schools have taken up a curriculum for the brighter streams that is geared to anything but getting to Oxford and Cambridge; and this has meant inevitably a preoccupation with dead languages. Latin and Greek have been encouraged on the largely bogus ground that they were education; judged by what they do to those who have read them this is patently untrue; it is reasonable to assume that Classics had a technical function of getting them into Oxford and Cambridge and keeping the others out. (The cradle of western civilization has become part of the public school 'tradition', till Athens seems a sort of pre-preparatory school, and Sparta a rugger pitch.) The preoccupation with Latin and Greek has been literally disastrous to many people whose contact with their own culture has atrophied; and it has grossly distorted a great deal of English education for intelligent children of all classes.

Perhaps the most disastrous effects of the public school system are not to be seen in—to take a few examples at random—Sandhurst, Cowdray Park, the Foreign Office, the Royal Academy and Dr. Fisher, but in what it does to the fringe public schools and bad grammar schools that try to keep up. A bad grammar school, with its traditions, its houses, its rugger, its uniform, its corporal punishment, its petty snobbery, its old boys, its seedy masters, is a monstrous parody of the better public schools.

What can we do about it? Just fulminate? It certainly seems impossible to do anything drastic, like abolishing them; the Labour Party is paralysed by the involvement of its leaders in their love-hate relationship with the public schools. Issues like parental 'freedom', the 'freedom' to spend money on schools and so on, bogus as they are, represent but the beginning of the furore that would be raised if a government tried to interfere seriously with the present set-up.

The only serious alternative so far proposed is that suggested in the Fleming Report. This is a scheme for enlarging the influence of public schools by recruiting a proportion (25 per cent) of their population by scholarship from local authorities. The objections to this are manifold. It leaves the public schools as they are. It imposes a frightening task of selection on education authorities, and in practice it would subsidise mainly middle-class children; probably those already there.

On the other hand it seems impossible to incorporate the public schools into the state system without radically and almost inevitably changing their character; above all, most suggestions would involve the abolition of fee-paying (thus imposing a burden on public funds) and retaining a problem of selection. In practice this would mean giving extra money on a very large scale to the bright; there seems an indissoluble problem arising from the small number of public school places and their high cost. Above all, people who are excluded from existing schools, although their parents could afford the fees, would swell the queues at lesser public schools, and so grossly inflate the system.

I think there is another way out.

There are two main difficulties in bringing public schools into the state system of education—selection and finance. How do you choose a tiny minority of boys and girls to be given an expensive education, and how do you justify so much expenditure? If we set ourselves three clear objectives, the answer is, I think, strikingly simple. The three objectives are: non-selectivity, economy and freedom to pay fees.

First, at a time when we are abolishing the 11-plus, it is clear that there should be no rigorous selection test for public schools. This prevents the adoption of a scheme involving selection at the age of 9, at 11 or at 13 because there are far too few places for all applicants. At 15, however, there are enough places in public and 'direct-grant' schools (taken together) for almost all the sixth formers in England, *provided that the children under 15 are excluded from these schools.* Thus selection can be virtually abolished if the public and 'direct-grant' schools take no children of less than 15; that is, roughly, if the first year of public school and the 'lower-school' of direct-grant schools is excluded from them.

The next objective is to finance the places in independent schools. If tuition were paid for state scholars who passed an examination and agreed to stay at school until they were 18, there could be a means test for the 'boarding' education and the 'extras' at day schools. (It is in fact likely that sixth-form education in grammar schools is just as expensive as in some 'direct-grant' schools.) Educational endowments can be attracted to these 'leadership' schools, as the £3½ million fund for science laboratories has shown; industry could be encouraged to give money to the schools which accepted the scheme, and prevented (to all intents and purposes) from giving money elsewhere by refusing tax reliefs on money given elsewhere. In other words, the extra cost to the state would not be very great.

The third objective is to leave parents free to spend money on education, and to leave people free to open schools if they want to, (provided the schools are up to certain minimum standards). This could be done by making a proportion of the places at all the public and 'direct-grant' schools available for fee-payers, and by enabling the endowment funds to be used to expand the schools. It should be possible, too, to restore fee-paying in some grammar schools by allowing them to opt for direct-grant status. Indeed, in order to bring the number of places into line with the demand probably a number of ordinary grammar schools would have to be given direct-grant status.

Thus our three objectives of non-selectivity, economy and freedom to pay, are achieved by three simple administrative devices: expanding direct-grant status *up* to the great public schools and *down* to the grammar schools; making direct-grant status conditional in providing substantially only upper-fifth and sixth form work; allowing a substantial element of fee-paying and attracting industrial endowments.

The mechanics of this scheme are simple, and they are enabled to be so because the analysis of the public schools has concentrated clearly on analysing their merits and their disadvantages.

Their great merits are those of good schools anywhere: an abundance of physical resources, small classes and excellent teaching. Their advantages spring, however, from their social exclusiveness, which divorces them from any genuine relationship with the rest of society. Most of their disadvantages can be traced to this single cause. They tend to be cut-off; they tend to have a mystique about leadership; they produce a marked type with originality reduced to a safe level. All previous schemes of reform have proposed, however, that the social exclusiveness should be replaced by a similar kind of exclusiveness based upon intelligence and 'character'. In practice, as socio-psychological studies have demonstrated, this would not seriously dilute the existing stream of moneyed children, and it would have the great disadvantage of opening up even more a prospect of a country governed by a 'meritocracy' chosen at 11. Furthermore, unless the spending of money on private education is forbidden there is always the possibility that just as many new places will be provided for fee-payers as are taken away from them by state action; thus doubling the system immediately and making the last situation worse than the first. As a practical policy there is little to be said for 'taking-over' the public schools unless they are changed.

Yet, if they are changed they may lose their character and both their good and their bad qualities might tend to disappear together, and this would not only be a misfortune but it would also cause a legitimate public outcry. The scheme suggested here tries to differentiate between what is good and what is bad.

In doing this, it must point to four things. First, a great deal of the trouble about public schools is that they do not consist entirely of senior boys, but have 'little boys' there as well. This enables 'leadership', 'corruption' and so on to be exercised; between the senior boys there is a degree of camaraderie that would be expected in a normal group of that age. Clearly, if we get the 'small' boys out, then some of the major disadvantages disappear.

Next, it is important to give an adequate sixth form education to all young people who are willing to ask for it. For many of them the sixth form should offer a chance of getting away from home, of adequate sports facilities, and of good libraries and—above all—intelligent teaching. In many small grammar schools these things are available; but rarely are they available on the scale that can be offered by the public schools; indeed, an additional test for a public school is that it should have a very large sixth form.

Yet the atmosphere of a day-school sixth form seems to be more liberal than that of a boarding school; and a sixth-form equivalent at a technical college or art school is even more 'liberated'. No uniform, smoking, dances and dating, no restriction on 'out-of-school' activities—these are all in striking contrast with public schools; and to my mind they are in very healthy contrast. (I shall always remember interviewing a boy from a small public school near London who was nearly 19 and had never been to a London theatre because he was not allowed out after six o'clock at night.)

Clearly, the efflux of small boys from the public schools would in itself ease the emphasis on 'boyhood' and allow the remaining students to be treated sensibly; above all, the influx of a substantial group of boys and girls of sixth-form age who were unbrainwashed would lead to some splendid questioning of the system as it stands. I anticipate with delight the arrival of some lively boys from L.C.C. grammar schools to question our friend who was 'so glad about A.A.N.T—'s M.B.E.' The new 'direct-grant' schools would therefore become the equivalent of the junior colleges that are so clearly needed in modern society.

This is the third important point to bear in mind. In contrast with North America and Russia, Britain has lagged in its provision of pre-university courses; it is the quantity of education (as well as the quality) that marks a highly-educated society, and it is because of ignorance of this fact that educational policy on the 'progressive' side of politics has lagged behind acknowledged social developments. The public and 'direct-grant' schools are the obvious nuclei for such a system, as the fee-paying parents have seen. They pay most for what is best, from the point of view of their children; and, for once, private and public interests tend to coincide in this matter.

This brings me to the fourth point that needs to be borne in mind differentiating between the good and the bad in the existing public schools. It is the element of fee-paying. Of itself, this is a good thing. It is valuable to have some element of contribution to the finance of education from those who can afford it; probably it adds to a sense of parental responsibility; and, above all, it makes the education system responsive, in some sense, to the expressed wishes of the parents. Clearly, however, fee-paying at present amounts to the purchase of social privilege (by making it easier, for instance, for children to go to the universities, or into the army as an officer) and it restricts the freedom of those with inadequate means. My suggested scheme has the great advantage of keeping both the independence of the schools and a large element of fee-paying.

In short, it is possible to envisage the relaxed system of sixth-form education, partly boarding, all well-equipped, coping with much of the sixth-form work in Britain. It could be expanded reasonably fast, as demand rose, and it would have a built-in system of subsidy from parental fees and contributions, and from industrial endowments. The masters would benefit from the removal of the 'little boys', and from having to deal with a socially more mature set of pupils, many of whom would be extremely critical of fundamentals. In such a situation good teaching flourishes.

What, however, of the rest? It is implicit in what has been said that many of the difficulties of integrating the public schools into society spring from the existence of prep-schools taking boys from 7 or 8 to 14. A blow would of course be struck at these by raising the age of admission to public schools; they would have to provide more education for the senior boys who were unable to leave. It is important to remember, too, that the expanded programme of 'secondary education for all' that is being undertaken is in direct competition with these schools (not with public schools) and that their popularity may wane. Yet the arguments for incorporating them into the public system are very strong: they are a potent source of the educational and social disasters that I have outlined and they are almost as much at the heart of the trouble.

It seems to be that once more a simple solution is to be found by the restoration of fee-paying at all schools; if any parent is dissatisfied with the school chosen for his children by the local education authority, then he should be free (within reason) to buy a place at any other school, public or private. As a corollary, all private schools should be required to offer a large proportion of their places to education authorities, and there should be a contribution for additional costs (such as boarding facilities) according to means. In any area where there was a surplus of places, the bad schools would be closed for lack of support because either the parents would be satisfied with the local authority schools, or they would force the authority (by their exercise of the right of fee-paying) to support other schools. Again, every private school should be required to have an endowment fund, and local authority schools would be free to seek endowment to increase their fee-income.

Above all, these suggestions seem to me to remedy one of the problems of the grammar school. Many of them are too small to support a really adequate sixth form but are sufficiently big to give really efficient teaching to children up to G.C.E. 'O' level. Further, in the cultural conditions of today sixth-formers are not on the whole content to be treated as schoolboys. They want to be treated separately. In fact, in many schools, the sixth form is almost a separate school from the rest, with its own rules and regulations, its own masters and its own games. Under this system a grammar school could choose to be a 'direct-grant' school or a 'high school' (to adopt a phrase now in vogue in the Ministry of Education). Immediately the problems of the 11-plus are eased; and the difficulties of the bad grammar schools are eased.

These suggestions are put forward in order to show a way out of an apparent impasse; in detail it is possible to vary them considerably. It is certain, however, that if it were impossible to maintain a school unless it could attract endowment and some public support, and if the age of admission to public schools were raised to 15, then some of the major problems revealed by the present system would be resolved.

What, after all, is one trying to do by suggesting schemes of change? Surely the answer in the main is to suggest where the present system falls down. If we look back at our picture of the public school boy—the typical public school boy, not his idealized model who takes the Fellowship at All Souls—we see certain general characteristics. One is a striking degree of uniformity of speech, dress, manners and values. This suggests that the degree of brainwashing has been alarming. In contrast with many state schools, the public school is working with masters, parents and pupils, who willingly accept all the values implicit in their social situation. This in itself is a dangerous situation; it is arguable that an educational system should shake people up.

Our study of the values implicit in the public school boys' behaviour showed them to be alarming, too. They are based, for better or worse, upon a highly conscious degree of class consciousness, and a conscious degree of superiority that in the marginal cases become snobbery, and in the others supercilious arrogance. It seems to me that many of the other false values are subsidiary to this main value.

Now, one way to break up this calm superiority or uncalm snobbery is considerably to dilute these schools with boys and girls from different backgrounds. But so strong are the forces that they exercise, so great is the pressure of conformity that they can bring to bear, that it is morally certain that the addition of a few—or even, possibly, a great many—children from other backgrounds will merely succeed in 'de-classing' the newcomers without changing the values themselves. It seems that the answer to this is to put the emphasis on the impact of older children from different backgrounds; the arrival of intelligent and non-conforming working-class children of 15 or 16 can do much. Above all, however, it is necessary to loosen-up the schools, to encourage them to look outwards at the world rather than to create a private world, and to remind them that their pupils are people, and people should be free much of their time from institutional claims.

It is this last assertion that will be most strongly contested. It has been a commonplace of educational discussion that a school is a microcosm; in it, the world's game can be played out in miniature; and all under the eye of benevolent rather than malevolent gods. Armed with the knowledge gained in a kind of spiritual link-trainer the pupils can go out into a real world and traverse its skies with confidence. This seems to me to be a pernicious doctrine. A school is not a microcosm. It is the antithesis, in some respects, of the world at large; it is, at most, a part of a child's environment. A child's most important relationships are with his family, then there is a growing series of relationships with the world at large of which his school is only part, and it may be a not very important part. Above all, children go to school to learn certain specific skills—reading, writing, computation, the use of language, and later languages, mathematics, science and the arts, as well as rugger, music and painting. Why to this there should be added 'character' and 'tradition' is rather mystifying, unless you specifically regard the school (as Arnold did) as a place where the harmful assumptions of society at large were to be eradicated and new values substituted.

At the time these values were heterodox. Now they are the orthodox assumptions of a ruling class. In a modern society there is no need for a ruling class; and much of recent history has suggested that it is, in fact, a handicap. Our Foreign Office, for example, is manifestly inferior to most; our armed services do not compare at all well with the United States and Canada; and the general level of public debate is much less informed and far more intolerant than that in the United States and some other countries. These characteristics are not unrelated to the conforming attitudes of many of our leaders; attitudes in which they were indoctrinated in early life and which are based upon an acceptance of a hierarchical model of society which seems an extremely unfortunate preparation for later life. Above all, perhaps, what strikes one about stories of children who are unhappy at school (and surely their evidence is among the most valuable) is that there seems to be no end to it; school takes up all their lives and they cannot escape to be themselves without running away or retreating into their shells.

Should not the young be left free to choose; to choose their friends, to choose their leisure, to reflect and choose their values. A pupil of mine who ran away from Shrewsbury (where he had gone by scholarship from a good grammar school) said that his day was entirely full; morning, noon and night there was always something on and he was never by himself unless the system specifically said that he *was* to be by himself. It all seemed, he said, so childish. There was, too, little respect for your essential personality; public school boys have little real sense of privacy; and this is because they are always being adapted and having their 'rough corners knocked off'. It is not surprising, my pupil tells me, that they knuckle down so well to National Service; but do we want a society of people who knuckle down to National Service? I am sure that we do not.

It seems to me then that on social grounds the system stands condemned; but it stands condemned on educational grounds, too.

Perish by the Sword

by *Simon Raven*

Novelist. Fiction critic of *The Spectator*. Sometime captain in King's Shropshire Light Infantry. Author of *The Feathers of Death*. Married, one son. Pagan.

THE sword is the emblem of military authority. Everyone in the Army has one, though the more important he is the more resplendent and generally impractical his sword will be. Private soldiers have bayonets—token swords, one might say, reminders of the immemorial origins of soldiering and what is even now the occasional necessity of killing face to face. Mounted troopers have crudely fashioned sabres. Regimental-sergeants-major, being of some grandeur, have proper swords with ciphered hilts—shorter than officers' swords, however, to remind the R.S.M. of his exact social status. Officers themselves have all kinds of swords: one kind in the Royal Regiment of Artillery, another in the Light Infantry, and claymores, of course, in the Highland Regiments; while general officers have swords with unguarded ivory hilts, weapons of great beauty and value. None of these, except for the common soldier's bayonet, ever appear now save only on ceremonial occasions. But they are still there for all that, kept bright by batmen for the annual parade, worn for the photographs that will be sent to housemasters and mothers. For the sword is the symbol not only of might but of leadership and honour; it denotes the righteous anger of the silver knight who rides against Saladin, the purity of St. George, above all, perhaps, the brave words spoken at Agincourt. . . . So that every now and again the old order still goes out: 'Officers will wear swords.' It is accepted as a duty and a privilege. But who are the young men who run upstairs to instruct their servants, "Tomorrow our swords must be bright —see to the sheathes and buckles"? What kind of man is it, in this year of grace 1959, who thinks to himself with pleasure as he prepares for bed, 'Tomorrow, like Hector or Achilles, I shall wear my sword'?

.   .   .   .   .

I bought myself a sword, one afternoon in the spring of 1953, from Messrs. Wilkinson of Pall Mall. I had had a heavy luncheon and so chose a badly balanced one, which was subsequently about as much use as Excalibur for taking on parades. But that, of course, was not the point. . . . For in a few weeks, having no money and nothing else to do, but anticipating travel and excitement and companionship, I was to rejoin the Army as a regular officer in the rank of lieutenant. As such, I must clearly have a sword. I certainly took it with me everywhere, until, in the autumn of 1957, a series of regrettable and squalid misunderstandings, all entirely due to my own fault, compelled me to tender a very hasty resignation. Thus I served some four and a half years with the colours—years upon which I look back with pleasure, affection, and even (except of course for the squalid misunderstandings) with pride. So while on the one hand this essay is based on experience in an Army from which I was, for all practical purposes, expelled, on the other hand any bias I have is firmly in the Army's favour. (This lest anyone should think that the conclusions I shall later draw are the result of disgruntlement or spite.) I propose to cast the essay itself in a roughly autobiographical frame, taking the observations I made as my career proceeded stage by stage and pointing, at the end of each stage, to certain deductions about the nature of the modern Army—deductions, however, which will be chiefly and indeed almost wholly concerned with the officers of that Army and the young officers at that. If this seems too deliberate a limitation, I can only say that I am writing an essay and not a book; and that since people are always abundantly ready to curse Army officers for anything that goes wrong, while in the public mind no blame can ever be attached to the rank and file, I can only presume that general belief really does accord to officers as a class the importance which they (and I) would accord themselves. As for my pre-occupation with young officers, it will be allowed that the secrets of the generals of 1984 are concealed in the subalterns of 1958. Finally, if the use of an autobiographical approach seems to denote self-centredness or self-satisfaction, I must reply that, since this essay is of necessity based on the personal observations of a serving officer and not on prolonged field work or statistical analysis, it is well that I should be honest about it and not pretend to a width of knowledge or objectivity of method that I cannot claim. All of which brings me back to the spring of 1953, when I waited eagerly for the word to join the Regimental Depot of the King's Shropshire Light Infantry and meanwhile read *The Shropshire Lad* to put me in good trim.

I was at this time twenty-five years old, had taken a fair degree in Classics at King's College, Cambridge, had travelled a little in Europe, and counted myself a man of culture and a man of the world. I had been in the immediately post-war Army before going up to Cambridge, but that had been an affair of flux and confusion —a vast, sprawling mass, which was really nothing but an inefficient machine for getting itself demobilized. By 1953, however, things had presumably settled down. National Service had come firmly in to stay, with predictable schedules and properly timed periods of training. Regular officers were again in the ascendant, the older ones having emerged from the indiscriminate war-time scrummage of acting and temporary ranks, the younger ones now appearing fresh from Sandhurst, where they took eighteen months instead of four to learn their business. Senior non-commissioned rank was by now confined almost entirely to long-service Regulars. Above all, I thought, there must surely by now be enough space and enough leisure for action to be dictated by thought and consideration instead of merely precipitated by the ill-informed nagging and abruptly exploding muddles typical of 1946. I should find, I told myself, organization and professional method—an Army and no longer a rabble. Again, it was, they said, as far as its officers were in question, a new kind of Army—different not only from that of 1939 to 1945, but also from that of before the war: no longer an established club for established people, or a useful repository for the slow-witted or superfluous members of Establishment families, but a new Army freed from the grip of social prejudice, in which only the meritorious could aspire to success or even to place. However this might be, it was a prospect full of interest, opportunity and promise. The event was to confirm my superficial and optimistic predictions, and was indeed to redouble my interest; but such interest was to assume a distinctly sinister nature, and it is this which I hope to convey in these pages.

.   .   .   .   .

The first thing I was made to do on rejoining the Army was to attend a junior officers' course at the School of Infantry at Warminster. This course was more properly intended for newly commissioned officers straight from Sandhurst, and was designed to provide them with such basic and practical knowledge of tactics and administration as they would require to command a platoon of infantry in the field or to assume temporary command of a company—a duty which devolves on extremely junior people more often than might be thought. If it seems curious that, after eighteen months spent training as cadets, these young officers should nevertheless require an immediate course in the most elementary techniques of their profession, I should explain that the training at Sandhurst is of an academic and very generalized nature. They say that a cadet leaves the R.M.A. with the theoretical knowledge needed to command a Division and with practical experience inadequate to dispose correctly of two men and a light machine-gun. However this may be, no matter what branch of the Army he is to enter, every cadet receives—or did receive—the same general training; and it is only after he is commissioned that he is instructed in the immediate and specialized requirements of his own arm. One result of this is that young officers, instead of proceeding immediately to active units where the normal make-shift arrangements of fallible humanity prevail, spend far too long in the sedate and perfected routines of Army 'Schools' and 'Institutions', where the instructors are smug and hand-picked and there are always enough blackboards. (This is never the case in an ordinary unit.) The young officers are shielded too long from the irritations and 'make do and mend' atmosphere of everyday soldiering. Still, there was a lot to be learned at Warminster, and it was certainly fitting that I, a university entrant who had not seen a rifle in five years, should find myself there as a student of the infantryman's basic and essential crafts.

To go into the details of these latter would be a bore to anyone who is not a specialist; but a brief discussion of the general virtues which the pundits of Warminster sought to inculcate is relevant. For these virtues are of cardinal importance, and until one understands them, one can never understand the British officer.

While much of the training was inevitably designed to promote physical fitness, there was nevertheless a strongly held belief that an officer, whether fit or not, should always have so much in the way of pride or 'guts' that he would never admit to physical inadequacy until he dropped dead or unconscious. This belief, a very significant one, was mystical both in its nature and intensity.

During a crippling exercise at the end of the course two or three officers fell out complaining of blisters or other mild indispositions. The Chief Instructor, himself a civilized and self-indulgent man, denounced them in round terms. An officer, he said, simply could not and did not fall out: will power, if nothing else, should keep him going for ever: it was all a matter of 'guts'. There was an unspoken implication that, since other ranks could and did fall out, even though they were often physically tougher, the officer belonged to a superior caste. As we shall see, I found it an accepted belief among officers later on that they could perform physical feats or endure physical discomforts without it being in the least necessary for them to train or prepare for such things in the manner required of the private soldier. Officers, for example, just did not do P.T.: they did not need it; they were officers and would endure to the very end, had they stepped straight on to the field from a sanatorium or a brothel. It was, after all, a simple matter of guts.

Considerations of this kind serve to show how much, in the last resort, was thought to depend on superior qualities of morality and character. Indeed, while the military arts were given precise attention, it was none the less the general catchwords with quasi-moral implications ('guts', 'common sense') that filled the air as the course went on. Another excellent example of the Warminster virtues was a peculiar brand of 'humour'. This was not the ability to see oneself and one's activities in a detached and ironical spirit —this would have been fatal. 'Humour' meant being cheerful in the face of unpleasant circumstances, rallying the men's spirits by laughing with them over some slapstick incident, submitting 'like a good sport' to an unjust punishment given to oneself by the Adjutant and 'laughing about it afterwards in the mess'. This conception of humour (an obvious branch of 'guts') was in fact discreetly designed to counteract or totally extinguish any tendencies towards an objective or intellectual humour that might contain tinges of satire or cynicism—for such a thing would have been detrimental to another highly prized virtue, that of 'enthusiasm'. About 'enthusiasm' I can hardly trust myself to speak. It seemed to mean a sort of blind, uncritical application to any task, however silly or futile, that the neurosis or panic of a superior might suddenly thrust upon one. Since one of the points of 'enthusiasm' was that you started doing whatever it was straight away and without wasting time on questions, 'enthusiasm' could involve a frantic expense of time and energy on some trifling project, wastefully because uncritically undertaken, abandoned half-way as irrationally as it was commenced. This, of course, was just what great soldiers of the past wished to avoid when they deplored the indiscriminate use of 'zeal'. Why zeal, condemned alike by von Clausewitz and Wellington, should now once again be thought desirable it is interesting to speculate. Myself I suspect that it is because a superior and analytical attitude is considered undemocratic; and that the influence of such people as Lord Montgomery has dictated a spirit, for junior officers at least, of 'mucking in' and 'getting on with the job'. The heartiness, not to say hysteria, implied by such expressions was of course distasteful to the more fastidious and sceptical officers, for whose benefit yet another virtue, that of 'loyalty', had to be invoked. Loyalty meant that you were required, in the name of the Queen and the honour of the Regiment, to conceal any impatience or amusement you might feel when the demands on your enthusiasm became operatic, farcical or just plainly impossible of fulfilment. Loyalty, in fact, was a conception often blatantly used to blackmail you into silence when you were faced with the incompetence, injustice or sheer folly of a superior officer.

'Sociability' was also highly esteemed at Warminster. This, like loyalty, *could* mean many good things, such as hospitality and the desire to please in social intercourse, but it also implied an unquestioning deference to the convenience and opinions of one's military superiors. That one should obey the orders of such superiors, or even be 'loyal' to them during displays of professional vapidity, is perfectly reasonable; but I could never discover why one should be expected, in a purely social context, to receive as gospel wisdom their views on anything from body-line bowling to revealed religion. Normally, politics and religion are eschewed in officers' conversation; but grounds for controversy still remain, and I have never forgotten the trouble I got into for contradicting a general who announced that 'sodomy had rotted the Roman Empire'. The fact that this officer scarcely knew a word of Latin and, by his own confession, had never read a line of Gibbon, was held to be irrelevant. The general had spoken, and so sodomy, for this occasion at least, had indeed rotted the Roman Empire, however Tacitus or Professor Adcock might opine.

'Courage under fire', a sort of distilled essence of 'guts', could not exactly be taught, and so had to be taken for granted in all of us, who were tacitly and grimly assumed to possess it. Hence we can pass to a very much boosted commodity—'initiative'. This meant (subject to orders received and unquestioning enthusiasm in the face of these) that oneself must always be ready to devise and sponsor an original course of action. A valuable military quality, most certainly: but unfortunately in peace-time conditions and even for the most part in war-time ones, communications are now so good and the opportunities for genuinely individual action so rare, that 'initiative' tends to become a highly contrived thing artificially fostered to impress superiors. It becomes, in fact, mere interference with the existing order of things which, to give an excuse for showing keenness and interest, are made out to be in some respect 'slack' or 'unsatisfactory'. A genuinely adventurous spirit is one thing, arbitrary exhibitions of officiousness are quite another; and the sort of person who was praised at Warminster for 'initiative' generally turned out to be a meddlesome bully of the type who reports his best friend to his housemaster for immoral behaviour—thereby himself becoming head prefect in his friend's place. Such interference, I need hardly say, is also taken to show 'responsibility', which is the last of the great Warminster virtues I wish to deal with here.

'Responsibility' is in a way the pivot of the whole system. Like the Holy Ghost, it is supposed to be everywhere, and anything which is not material for the exercise of guts, enthusiasm, or one of the other Warminster qualities, will certainly turn out to be in the realm of 'responsibility'. Furthermore, even when a situation specifically requires guts, enthusiasm or whatever, it is ten to one that it will require a strong admixture of 'responsibility' as well. 'Responsibility' is thus twice blessed. It invades the spheres proper to all other qualities and it has a large kingdom in which it rules alone. It covers everything from making an intelligent assessment of how to move a Division, down to being careful not to get drunk in the sergeants' mess. It means not gambling for high stakes, not being late for parade, not sending reports to the Press, and not going to bed with your company commander's wife—however pressingly invited. In fact it is a very negative asset in many ways and, though assisting dignity and self-control, often turns out to be a stultifying nuisance.

So much for the teaching at Warminster. Technical military method was competently and thoroughly dealt with, but it was all, in a manner, seen to be subordinate to and dependent upon the great moral and quasi-moral imperatives: guts and almost mystical pride in officer status, humour (of the rugger club variety), enthusiasm and loyalty, sociability, courage, initiative and responsibility. And the greatest of these is responsibility. I have tried to indicate the slant which our instructors gave these qualities for their specific purpose, and in so doing I may have oversimplified and caricatured: broadly speaking, however, I believe that what I have been saying conveys an honest estimate of the moral force of our instruction. It will be appreciated, of course, that such instruction had a distinctly Establishment ring about it—most notably in the conception of an officer's automatic ability to suffer hardship, an ability which was supposedly derived from the mere fact of being an officer. However 'new' the Army was, however many potential officers it might have recruited from outside normal Establishment circles, the virtues it wished its new entry to possess were of a long-established nature. But mention of the 'new' entry brings us to another question: who were the young men that received this instruction? where did they come from? and in what state of education and maturity were they when, having just received the Queen's Commission, they came to the School of Infantry at Warminster?

.   .   .   .   .

At the outset, I must remind the reader that all these boys were infantry officers. What difference it would have made if they had been a selection of cavalrymen, gunners or engineers, it is difficult to say. Probably cavalrymen are richer and come in the main from better established families, gunners are more or less on a par with infantrymen, while engineers and officers of the more technical corps are, from the point of view of money or social class, the inferiors of the average young man I met at Warminster. Still, though it is only infantrymen I am writing about here, the social range of Infantry Regiments, from the Foot Guards to obscure Regiments of the Line, is so broad that what I shall say inevitably has a general relevance to the Army as a whole.

There are for practical purposes three ways of obtaining a Regular Commission: directly from a university, by transition from a National Service Commission, and by completing the course at the Royal Military Academy at Sandhurst. The latter method is by far the most common. Again, admission into Sandhurst is achieved in one of two ways: by passing an examination and a special board (the Regular Commissions Board) while still at school, or by being strongly recommended while actually serving as an other rank and, once more, passing the Regular Commissions Board. For obvious reasons the former (and larger) class of boy tends to be younger, better educated and more socially acceptable (to speak from the average officer's point of view), while a recommendation from the ranks indicates that the person thus recommended has either been too stupid or too badly educated to pass an extremely simple examination. Most of the officers I knew at Warminster had qualified for Sandhurst while still at school; but then again, though now such boys would go straight to the R.M.A., in those days they were pushed off to do a few months as rankers in some ordinary training establishment first, probably the respective depots of the regiments they hoped to join as officers. Even so, however, it was of course known in these establishments that such and such boys were destined for Sandhurst, so that, though they were possibly treated even more roughly than the average recruits, potential officers were segregated from the others in their accommodation and training and thus early made conscious of being different from everyone else. In fact the rough treatment specifically dished out to potential officer squads at Regimental Depots was often the pride both of the instructors and the squads themselves. When the members of such a squad returned as officers, the bond between themselves and their former N.C.O. instructors was of a curious emotional kind, in that it was forged out of the assumption, *by both parties*, that officer status had conferred something splendid and unique on the one-time pupils and so, by reflection, on their instructors. Here again one runs up against the almost mystical pride, of which I have already spoken, in the mere fact of being an officer—a pride which is fostered from the first day a recruit is set apart in a 'potential officer squad'.

But of course, to be set apart was exactly what such boys really expected (though they were none the less delighted when it actually happened). For all of them were immensely superior —and knew it—in class or education or both, to the normal recruit. This brings us to the schools attended by these boys before they joined. As far as the infantry is concerned, the correspondence between regiments and certain educational scales is almost mathematically exact, for since the war and the hopeless confusion of social values the question of a boy's social suitability is assumed, for the sake of simplicity, to depend largely on the school he attended. The only other substantial consideration is the private means which some regiments require their officers to possess—this despite the objection of Socialist Ministers of War. Thus to join a Regiment of Foot Guards it is preferable to have been at Eton, Winchester or Harrow, though one would be tolerated if one had been at another of the 'big six' public schools or one of the more reputable Roman Catholic concerns. It is also either essential or very desirable to have at least £150 a year of one's own. To go slightly downward in the scale, to be commissioned in one of the Rifle Regiments requires an almost similar educational status, though there is less direct emphasis on Eton, Harrow or Winchester: again, the Rifle Regiments are said to worry less about private money, though some of the officers are extremely rich. After this we descend to the Regiments of Light Infantry and Fusiliers. Here it is broadly true to say that, while it is almost essential to have been to a public school, it does not matter if it was a pretty shoddy public school: equally, it is exceptional for grammar school boys to be accepted. Being myself in the King's Shropshire Light Infantry, I well remember very harsh things being said when another Light Infantry regiment accepted as Regulars two boys of aggressively grammar school origin. But when it comes to private money at this level, its possession, while considered pleasant and desirable, is in no way stipulated.

After the Light Infantry and the Fusiliers, if we omit the Highland Regiments (which no Englishman in his right mind can begin to comprehend), we come to the absolutely plain run of Regiments of the Line. Such regiments are variable in calibre: but it would be true to say of many of them that they are consciously and purposefully *middle class* in their methods of selection—they might almost prefer, that is, a boy from Oundle to a boy from Eton, and often regard the possession of private means as unfair and even immoral. In such regiments private tastes for drinking and gambling are closely watched and commented upon, while homosexuality, for example, which, though scarcely encouraged, is not uncommon in regiments of a smarter and more worldly tone, would be considered profoundly shocking. (The degree of censorship passed on private morals is always a good indication of a regiment's social status: in 'Etonian' regiments moral comment is seldom heard, whereas the further down the scale we go, the more grindingly insistent it becomes.) Obviously middle-class regiments of this nature (quite apart from the fact that the supply of public school boys may by now be running low) are quite content to absorb grammar school boys of industrious character from poor but moral homes. And so it falls out. In some ordinary Line Regiments as few as 20 per cent of the officers may be grammar school boys; but in many others the figure is 80 per cent or even higher. No names, no pack-drill. I should add that the very few Jewish boys who go in for soldiering find it difficult to get into the 'smarter' regiments; and that boys from secondary technical schools, while they would undoubtedly be acceptable in Infantry Regiments of the poorer class, go mainly and very sensibly to technical regiments—the Signals, R.E.M.E., and so forth. From all of which, two deductions are very plain. Though potential infantry officers from non-established or only semi-established circles are tolerated and indeed welcomed, they are nevertheless uncompromisingly denied admittance to the most glittering of the Establishment's *Salles Privées*. It is unthinkable that a grammar school boy should hold a Regular Commission in the Grenadier Guards, and that is that. Equally, however, there is no doubt that such a boy will easily be received into the dingier corners of the Establishment ('In my Father's house are many mansions'), provided that he is of suitable material to be stamped with the imprimatur of that particular branch. New lamps, in fact, are bought in bulk from the emporium and then carefully rigged up to assume the aspect of genuine antiques. Even so, they will not be placed in prominent positions in St. James's Palace; but they may well come to decorate creditable drawing-rooms in Camberley or York.

Now from all this a fairly plain pattern is beginning to emerge. Certain boys at public or secondary schools of every class get it into their heads that they want to be officers. They pass an examination and they pass a Regular Commissions Board—this when they are about eighteen. Thus they are already 'set apart'. Some of them, even at this early stage, have already been accepted as future officers in definite regiments: others know pretty well for which regiments their schools and pockets qualify them: while even the poorest boys from the most obscure schools know that there is a whole ruck of perfectly adequate regiments which require boys of keenness and good character, and that they only have to keep their noses clean to find a billet somewhere. They all have this in common—that they have *already* proved themselves fit, by qualifications of education and character, to hold commissions and exercise command. They are cut out to give the orders. If they are still in any doubt about their 'apartness', such doubt is speedily set at rest the first day they join the Army, by the instant recognition of their potential officer status, and their consequent disposal in separate and superior squads. A few months later, having been the cherished centre-piece of a regimental depot, they proceed to Sandhurst. They are now officer cadets: they are addressed as 'Sir' by all non-commissioned ranks (though they themselves have to return this compliment to the more senior of such ranks): they carry nice little canes: they have a specially designed uniform: some of them even have swords. Let us consider what happens to them now.

These days potential officers start their careers, not at a regimental depot or other ordinary training establishment, but actually at Sandhurst itself. However, for the first few months their position there is precisely the same as that of the boys I knew who themselves had to start elsewhere—they are taken to be raw recruits (with a difference) and treated as such, until the day comes when they are admitted to the Academy proper as fully fledged cadets. This is the stage we have now reached. Initial and basic training, whether conducted at Sandhurst or elsewhere (and in either case creating 'apartness' from the common soldier) is over. The education proper to an officer is now about to begin.

I think this may most conveniently be divided into three categories: the military category, which is a broad and general education in all military matters, ranging from the privileges of generals to the internal organization of a Divisional H.Q.; the academic category, which is the study of a certain number of humane or scientific subjects; and the character-building category, which is really of the greatest interest to us here.

To deal firstly and briefly with the specifically military side of the cadets' education, I can best describe this by saying that it is a general introduction to the whole trade of soldiering. It covers the characteristics, functions and organizations of the various arms and formations. Military Law comes in for some attention, as does the theory of discipline and man-management. Strategy and tactics are in evidence, the latter illustrated by fairly arduous practical exercises, but, as I have said before, such things are taught in a rather grandiose fashion, and the earthy business of handling a platoon or a section is hardly emphasized. (There is also a great deal of drill, though this is better discussed later as a feature of character-building.) All this is taught by highly qualified officers of irreproachable private lives. There is no doubt that a cadet who pays a modicum of attention can emerge from Sandhurst with a formidable knowledge of the disposition and administration of the British Army at all levels and in all its functions. In short, the military teaching is a model of efficiency and comprehensiveness.

Again, I have nothing but praise for what I know of the academic side of Sandhurst education. This is conducted by university graduates who have taken high honours. There is a reasonable element of choice, so that each boy can incline towards his bent; but there is a pardonable tendency to get the cadets to concentrate on the physical sciences or modern languages. It is noteworthy that in the teaching of the latter the literary side, so far from being played down, is accorded sympathy and emphasis. The cadets are strongly encouraged to travel during their ample vacations; expeditions of a cultural or semi-cultural nature are not uncommon; and some of the civilian instructors play a civilizing part in the cadets' lives comparable to what one might expect from a young and friendly don in a university. All this leads to improvement of manners, a general breadth of outlook and considerable mental flexibility. These admirable results of a liberal education were easily observed in the young man I met at Warminster; but I should add that such qualities in junior officers do not always give unalloyed pleasure to older men, reared in the more Spartan pre-war Sandhurst tradition, who maintain that such liberality of outlook is often at odds with the less compromising type of military requirement. But for that matter, the character-building side of a cadet's education is deliberately designed, in many respects, to offset any sceptical or easy-going attitudes that might result from so broad an education. The official theory (a product of the immediately post-war era) is that strict discipline and liberal education can complement and strengthen each other; in practice they are often plainly opposed, and serious friction between the civil and military instructors is not unknown. All of which brings us to the last and most interesting category of Sandhurst education—that which is concerned with character and discipline, if you like with the moral formation of the cadet.

In some ways, of course, this resembles the moral instruction subsequently dealt out at Warminster and already described here. The main difference is that, whereas at Warminster the qualities to be desired are to a great extent generalized and treated as a frame of reference, at Sandhurst there is a practical and immediate application of a lot of practical and immediate rules to obtain a series of concrete and immediately apparent results. Thus it is not so much a matter of talking about 'enthusiasm' (though no doubt people do) as of simply making the cadets run everywhere. It is less a matter of preaching 'responsibility' in general than, for example, of dishing out a severe punishment to a cadet who overdraws by one halfpenny the 'nursery' banking account which every boy is compelled to keep within the Academy itself. This practical type of character-building (Arnoldian in essence) is, in the last resort, the staple of Sandhurst education, and I now propose to give some examples of the method as it is applied there.

The 'prefect' system, I need hardly say, is almost viciously in evidence. There is in fact a complete cadet hierarchy which ranges from cadet lance-corporals to cadet under-officers and which runs parallel to the hierarchy of real officers and N.C.O.s actually on the instructing staff. Minor matters of discipline and administration are left to these cadet officials, and it is interesting to consider the powers they enjoy. Cadet N.C.O.s can bring charges against other cadets and the more officious are not slow to do so. A senior under-officer, who is of course no older than the boys he disciplines, is empowered to deal with such charges at his own 'Orderly Room', at which he may inflict quite heavy punishments, in the form of extra drills, on minor offenders. Beyond the mere exercise of such concrete powers, cadet N.C.O.s and particularly the under-officers are charged with maintaining the 'tone' of their own company, and this opens up a vast realm of semi-official influence and interference. I have heard of U.O.s who kept a strict watch on the private studies or sexual morals of other cadets and did not neglect to report their more significant discoveries to higher authority. A good company commander will discountenance such activities in his U.O.s: less sensible men may even encourage them. The seriousness and good character of non-public school cadets often effects their promotion to such positions, where their ignorance of public school notions about 'sneaking', their exemplary consciences and their desire to improve their already inflated status can bring about inquisitions and tyrannies of a most sinister kind. Some U.O.s go power mad. I know of one who used to visit people's rooms, throw their carefully polished best boots out of the window, and then order that the boots should be produced in five minutes' time, properly cleaned for his inspection. This kind of thing is mercifully rare: most U.O.s spend an unhappy time doing a thankless job which they are relieved to shed at the end of the course. Still, this particular system and the firm belief in it held by most of the instructors are outstanding features of the R.M.A. in its character-building role. The amount of 'responsibility', 'initiative' and pride in status churned out this way, not to mention the probability of less desirable effects, may easily be imagined.

Another Arnoldian touch is the ruthless way in which the cadets' private time and personal activities are restricted. These boys are the same age as undergraduates. Their routine of compulsory games, compulsory dining-in or compulsory private study would make the average undergraduate, or indeed the average private soldier of the same age, hysterical with rage and frustration. But it is not considered desirable for a cadet, during term time, to have private interests, and there is an end of it. The emphasis is on corporate life and corporate activity ('sociability' in its least compromising and attractive form). As for the games, apart from ensuring that the cadet is in a known place at a known time, they are also credited with bestowing the usual benefits—team spirit, *mens sana in corpore sano* and what not. But if fitness is a paramount consideration, self-control is even more so. This is where we finally arrive at that monumental institution, inescapable, lowering, nightmarish, implacable—the Drill Square. The amount of time cadets spend in performing complex (and very beautiful) drill movements, with perfectly timed co-ordination of feet and weapons, is scarcely credible. Drill is the special province of the warrant officers and, at the time of which I write, was above all the concern of that quintessential guardsman, Regimental-Sergeant-Major Lord. Mr. Lord, some say, is the most magnificent soldier in the world: beautifully proportioned, splendidly accoutred, with the eyes and wits of Ulysses, the voice of Agamemnon, the heart (for use only off the Drill Square) of Andromache, R.S.M. Lord on his rostrum was indeed a demi-god to inspire fear or adoration. Behind him would be the Adjutant (boots and spurs, breeches and sword) and behind him again perhaps the Commandant himself with the scarlet gorgets and hat-band appropriate to his unassailable rank. And beneath them the hundreds of cadets would wheel and turn, march and counter-march, with immaculate precision. It was a proud thing, they tell me, to drill under Sergeant-Major Lord, even though the slightest piece of inattention would send you whirling off the square under escort to await inevitable and heavy punishment, even though you drilled for hours on end until the stink of sweat and exhaustion hovered over the massed cadets like the brimstone over Sodom.

And of course, with such a man about the place, standards of dress (civilian or uniform) were superb. Appear turned out in the manner of the average business man going to his office this morning, and you would spend the rest of the term doing drills and restrictions. Again, the saluting at Sandhurst is tremendous. If you walk round Sandhurst looking remotely as if you might be an officer, you will receive an incessant barrage of compliments. The muddy boy in P.T. shorts will stop running, square his shoulders, and snap his eyes in your direction like knives. The elegant young gentleman in the brown trilby will lift it from his head with a controlled jerk to replace it an exact number of seconds later at precisely the same angle. Boys in uniform with sticks, swords, rifles or sub-machine guns will perform a volume of intricate movements, alone or as a body, for your especial benefit. Your bewilderment, pleasure or embarrassment mean nothing to them: it is merely a matter of correct compliments being paid at all times. . . . So go to Sandhurst in a bowler hat and see how the boys salute. Do not forget to return the salutes: in the face of such punctilious virtuosity, it is the least you can do.

That is all I am going to say about the character-building side of Sandhurst. The elements involved are simple enough: they are direct and practical, and are calculated to impress, in an immediate, physical and memorable way, the virtues of responsibility, obedience, physical proficiency and self-control, politeness to superiors, and the forfeiture of personal pleasure and convenience in the face of corporate demands. But before I go on to summarize the conclusions towards which I have so far been working (the conclusions I reached when at Warminster after a study of the young officers there), I should make one further observation. The characters, intelligences, general abilities, of most boys who opt for the Army are, in relation to their educational backgrounds, of a very average nature. Brilliant boys do not go into the Army—they become lawyers, writers, dons or confidence men, but not soldiers. Nor do exceptionally stupid or sluggish or morally feeble boys: they would not pass a Regular Commissions Board. Sandhurst boys, in fact, are basically clean, amiable, reasonably intelligent, physically sound, medium-sensual human beings. Having said which, let us consider the picture as it now stands.

. . . . .

We have got our young men as far as the junior officers' course at Warminster. They have been commissioned for some weeks, but it will be some time more before they join their respective regiments for real, live soldiering. We have seen that they were boys of average intelligence and abilities who attended schools ranging from Eton to the lowliest grammar school, but all of whom have, in a fashion, enjoyed educational advantages. We have seen them selected, while still at school, by board and by examination, to undergo training as potential officers. We have seen them 'set apart' from other soldiers during their early training. We have seen them at Sandhurst subjected to competently administered military instruction, sound and even liberal academic instruction, but, above all, to moral and disciplinary instruction of a strict and confining nature. It has been tempting to wonder how far the liberal side of their education has balanced or even counteracted the disciplinary side, but we have as yet come to little conclusion about that—beyond remarking that they have pleasant manners and seem tolerably broad-minded. We know that they have been accepted for certain regiments on the strength of the schools they attended and the money they possess; and we know that some of these regiments, the 'smarter' ones from a social point of view, boast a more worldly and less moral air than the more 'middle class' and dingy Regiments of the Line.

In any event, here they are at Warminster, where they are being subjected to further influences which we have also considered in some detail in the early pages of this essay. We have seen that they are receiving at Warminster a good deal of military instruction, more specialized and detailed than that given at Sandhurst, to fit them for their particular job as infantry officers. But we have also seen that the emphasis is, if anything, far more strongly on certain qualities of morality and character. These qualities they were first introduced to at Sandhurst, but only, as it were, in a very primitive and *ad hoc* way: the qualities are now more disembodied, no longer the simple material for immediate nagging followed by summary punishment, but the magical stuff out of which they are expected to construct an ethos if not a religion. These qualities are shown as being fundamental to their lives and everything they do, as essential to their careers and very survival as officers. Military knowledge is one thing; but without the necessary pride in one's status and the determination never to prejudice that status by physical failure, without the 'humour' to disregard inconvenience and discomfort, the 'sociability' to be polite to superiors who are making fools of themselves, without the enthusiasm, courage, initiative and responsibility to see an action fiercely undertaken and reliably completed, military knowledge is mere vanity, sounding brass or tinkling cymbal. Thus spake the Chief Instructor. But what did all this mean to the amiable, well-disciplined, well-disposed adolescents whom he was instructing? How would they interpret all this as a guide for future action? 'All this', it must be remembered, had come on top of considerable previous training, training liberal and illiberal, military and cultural and moral—not to mention the careful impression of 'apartness' which had been steadily fostered in them for three years now. So how was this intricate matrix of instruction and training and influence to resolve itself in the finished product, the active officer when finally delivered to his regiment?

Obviously one was only to discover the answer to this when one arrived at such a regiment and saw for oneself how these young men and their immediate predecessors were to develop and acquit themselves. In the next and final stage of this essay, I shall try to describe just that—I shall try to show how, in my observation and judgement, these young men, so much belaboured with instruction and influence, in fact conduct themselves in the British Army of today—your Army and mine. Meanwhile, however, before going to my regiment, it was curious and instructive to speculate, on the grounds of what I had already seen and heard, about what I was likely to find. I thought I should find a self-consciously professional caste of officers, for such elaborate and extended training must surely encourage professional feeling: I thought that some officers, particularly in the 'Etonian' regiments, would be snobbish in a conventional, *Daily Mirror* baiting, way; and I was very much afraid that there would be a good deal of moral priggishness in my own regiment and others of the same kind—in which, I thought, there would not be enough upper class worldliness to counteract the sober strictures of Sandhurst and Warminster. But the important point is that I expected to find everything ultimately dependent on a purely *professional* attitude: I expected that professional knowledge, informed and strengthened by so much moral teaching, would result in a sense of professional obligation: I expected that the officers' claim to authority and command would be based on a professional sense of professional status attained as a result of professional qualifications and the professional training I have been at pains to describe. I cannot say I was much attracted by this conception, for it implied a sense of dedication which I felt might be both sinister and harmful; but at least it would be professional dedication, and therefore, to the Army at least, beneficial. All this, on the strength of what I had seen and learnt, I expected to find when I joined my regiment. In the event, the reality I found was something totally different. This reality, though superficially more amiable, was in essence far more sinister than the conception I had reached in my deductions. It too was completely deducible from what I had so far observed, but only if one gave logic the necessary slant which one should always give it when dealing with human and therefore fallible entities. I had neglected to give my logic this slant, and therefore what I was now to find, though utterly consistent, from a human point of view, with what I had already found, was a surprise of a staggering nature. So now we will leave military schools and institutions and go to see a little proper soldiering; and I shall try to make plain the very odd and sinister mystique by which I found it to be dominated.

.   .   .   .   .

I propose to begin by relating a small but indicative incident. When my battalion disembarked at Mombassa in the summer of 1955, we were to proceed as a unit by train to Nairobi—a journey of nearly twenty-four hours. When such a thing happens in England or Europe, officers travel first class and other ranks third class (as it then was), an efficient practical method of keeping people where you want them and one which provides the troops with accommodation, admittedly less comfortable than that of the officers, but perfectly adequate for all that. Feeding on such occasions is centrally organized: either everyone has sandwiches, or there is a dining-car in which the whole battalion eats by shifts. In the light of all this, the troop train from Mombassa was rather a surprise. There was a first class coach for the officers, and an ingenious system of couchettes provided each officer with a proper bed for the night. Next to the officers' coach was a well-appointed dining-car, in which we were provided with three hot meals during the journey and as much drink, within elastic licensing hours, as we could hold or pay for. Again, next to the dining-car was a second class coach for warrant officers and sergeants. This was perceptibly inferior to our first class affair, but it was tolerable to say the least and also had a workable system of couchettes. The warrant officers and sergeants had the use of the dining-car, and they, like ourselves, had three hot meals between Mombassa and Nairobi and a speedy bar service. Beyond this second class coach was a series of third class coaches 'for corporals and below'. These had wooden seats (very crowded wooden seats), bad ventilation, inadequate space for the men's kit, poor sanitation and execrable lighting. They were dirty in the extreme. There was not enough of them. (I was the wretched officer who had to try to pack everyone into them.) They were, in a word, unutterably bloody. And of course, there was no question of 'corporals and below' having a dining car. *Their* rations for twenty-four hours were two bags each (there were not, in any case, enough bags to go round) of stale sandwiches and half-rotten tomatoes.

I shall never forget the scene I found when, as 'train Adjutant', I had to accompany the R.S.M. down the train during the night. We could hardly get down the train for a start. Piles of kit, piles of bodies blocked everything. The smell of sweat was appalling, the stench from the blocked W.C.s purgatorial. The remains of the sandwiches and rotten tomatoes were encrusted over every-

thing and everybody. It was as I have always imagined D.P. trains
—rumbling away through Russia or Poland with their massed and
brutalized cargo—except that instead of cold there was a damp,
fetid, charnel-house heat. 'Corporals and below' did not have a
nice journey. I wonder we reached Nairobi without a mutiny.

I should emphasize, lest it be thought that I am having a cosy
leftist whine about this, that these conditions were not normal and
could never be found in Europe. This was Kenya, there was still
an emergency there, and in any case the authorities responsible
for our train, accustomed to make such very divergent arrangements for officers (all white) and other ranks (all coloured) when
transporting native regiments, had merely equated our troops for
this purpose with African askaris and provided the ferocious
accommodation deemed apposite by this reckoning. There was
no malice here, not towards us at any rate, only muddle. Our own
officers, who were in no way to blame for this, who had indeed
been trained to keep their men as happy as possible in all circumstances, were indignant and dismayed about this treatment of their
troops and did everything possible to improve their lot. But—and
here we reach the heart of the matter—there was one other element
in the attitude of our officers (and of course myself) which is not
so much cause for congratulation and in which the real significance
of this incident lies. "It was disgraceful," we said, "that the Kenyan
Government, when availing itself of the services of a famous
regiment, should think it could pack our men like cattle into such
foul transport. . . . But this much one must say for the Kenyan
Government, it had had the sense to realize that *gentlemen* could
not be treated in any way but the proper fashion. The arrangements for the troops were a disgrace, but at least a proper distinction had been made. And was it not now time for a drink and some
dinner? It was only to be hoped that the Kenyan Government
knew that gentlemen drank wine from France and not some
trumped-up muck from South Africa."

Now the point about such an attitude is this. We were *not*
saying that, as officers responsible for troops, we should automatically have better accommodation which would be consistent
with our official positions and enable us to perform our official
duties with more convenience and therefore more efficiency. We
were saying that since we were not only officers but also gentlemen
we were clearly entitled to be properly looked after and woe betide

the Kenyan Government if it dared forget the fact. The troops were our troops and their transport was a thoroughly poor show: they were still only troops and, at a pinch, must put up with this sort of thing. But we—well, we were gentlemen, and that was all there was to it. It is this particular aspect of officers' self-regard that I want to describe and explain in the last part of this essay. I want to make plain how little the average officer regards himself as a professional man giving orders by virtue of his professional status, and how strongly such an officer is convinced, despite the fact that his origins may be middle class or even lower in the social scale, that he has somehow been given the absolute and *personal* right to command, that this right is somehow rooted in himself as a person as firmly as such a right was deemed to be rooted in a feudal overlord, albeit for very different reasons. After my account of the education and moral training of a young officer, it may seem incredible that he should regard himself as exercising his powers by personal right, but that is exactly what I am saying does in fact happen. Indeed, I also hope to show that such an attitude, so far from being at variance with an officer's education, is the foreseeable and logical consequence of it. So let us now examine what is, in a sense, the feudal nature of the contemporary officer; and let us trace, if we can, the steps by which an education, supposedly professional in essence and sponsored, after all, by a democratic country, is positively creating from nothing a kind of feudal aspiration in an utterly incongruous class of young man.

The word 'feudal' has always been loosely applied to the Army, but most people mean by this only that the discipline is strict, or that officers are rather snobbish, or that there is no trade union. I am using the word in a far more exact sense—to mean, as the Oxford Dictionary says, 'based on relation of vassal and superior', based, that is, on a definite and unassailable personal right, which in the Middle Ages was conferred by social class and land tenure, but of course these days is conferred by other (equally artificial) considerations. Once a man arrogates to himself a 'feudal' right to command, it means he thinks he commands by right not only soldiers over whom he is appointed an officer but anyone who happens to belong to an inferior order. Once this matter of superiority and inferiority was very simply determined by reference to a strict scale of social precedence. The factors in the 'neo-feudalism' which I am trying to describe are very different. I think the best way to get an understanding of this 'neo-feudalism', its factors and its operation, is by considering certain basic examples of it as displayed in people I knew.

Second Lieutenant A. was a Roman Catholic from a professional family of moderate means—his father being a lawyer in a provincial town. He had done badly at Sandhurst, since he had a limited intelligence and little application, but he had a family connection with our regiment, was an agreeable and well mannered boy, and so was accepted by our colonel. He was sincere in his religious beliefs, but apt to drink too much and be sexually indiscriminate. His other amusements were horses (both racing and hunting), field sports in general, and enthusiastic but not high gambling. Here are some of the things which A. would not do because he considered them inconsistent with his status. He would not: be punctual with inferior ranks (*'they* wait for *me'*); join the troops in a run ('I don't need that sort of thing'); box with the troops ('they will not respect me if they see me with a bloody nose'); use the troops' lavatories, undertake any menial task (even on manoeuvres), or accept a dressing-down from a superior who, a survival from the war, had been commissioned after many years in the ranks. It is only fair to add that A. had a real gift for handling men and was outstanding on forest patrols in Kenya.

The point is beginning to emerge. A.'s conception of his status had nothing to do with his actual position or obligations as an officer or with good-form middle-class notions of proper conduct —in fact his ideas if anything compromised the former and ran completely counter to the latter. His conception of his position was definitely based on a type of feudal relation with his men.

Or consider Lieutenant B. Also trained at Sandhurst, B. had a first class analytical intelligence, fair general culture, and a liberal outlook in moral and social matters. The laziest man I have ever met, he had obviously only drifted into the Army by sheer chance and the lack of positive interest in any other idea when his parents suggested Sandhurst. B.'s amusements were reading, desultory conversations of a mildly philosophic nature, mathematics and bridge. He was utterly indifferent to the Army and everything about it, but his abnormally acute intelligence enabled him, despite his sloth, to get through his duties without any trouble. In fact B. was one of the few people I knew who never made a major blunder. Here are some remarks he made to me at various times:—

"Sergeant-Major X. took me on one side today and said my untidiness made a bad impression in the company. I told him that tidiness was only essential to the rank and file, who would otherwise just let themselves go altogether."

"Driver Y. didn't want me to drive his truck, so I drove it at seventy for five miles flat. It's good for them to see a little officer-type driving."

"Sergeant Z. is getting familiar. He asked me into his quarters for a cup of tea with his wife."

The pattern is becoming familiar. A kind and intelligent man, B. is nevertheless convinced that he cannot take tea with a sergeant's wife. If this had been mere petty snobbishness, it would have been disagreeable but harmless. It was, however, something far deeper: it was a genuine conviction of rooted and superior status which simply would not brook such a proceeding.

Or again, we have the very significant case of Temporary Captain C. C. had been in the very first intake at Sandhurst when it re-opened on a proper post-war basis and was thus older and more mature than A. or B. Unlike either of them, he was interested in the professional aspects of soldiering, and since he had a sharp intelligence allied with a subtle humour and a calm disposition, he spent much time and effort devising new ways of shortening cumbrous military processes, generally tedious matters of adminis-tration, and thus conferred a distinct benefit on our unit and his own men in particular. Indeed, C. was always very concerned with his men's welfare, to which he gave genuine consideration, and it would not be too much to say that, on the face of it, he was just the kind of competent, thoughtful and public-spirited young officer which a Labour Government would wish to perpetuate in a democratic Army. Further investigation, however, would have disclosed sentiments in C. of a scarcely democratic nature. "They are rather like pet animals," he said to me of his men one day; "one must keep them clean and properly fed, so that they do not get diseased and are in good working order. One must teach them to react swiftly and without thought to certain external stimuli or signals. Just as you whistle for a dog, so there must be certain simple and easily recognizable forms of words for the men. They must be given a certain amount of genuine affection, so that they feel loved and secure. They must expect, and on the whole receive, justice—a lump of sugar when they have done well, a whipping when they have been disobedient. But they must also realize that there are too many of them for justice always to work dead correctly in individual cases, and that occasional lumps of sugar will go to the idle and mischievous, occasional whippings to the industrious and innocent. . . . And they should be made to recognize the signs one sometimes gives when one simply does not want to be bothered with them."

Last of all, we might take a rather remarkable incident which features a certain Captain D. D., though ultimately of the same middle class stock as the others, had been at one of the 'top' public schools (though not Eton), had rather more money than the rest of us, and boasted a father who had served, during the war, in a regiment distinctly smarter than our own. Thus he had certain social pretensions, and it may have been these, rather than 'neo-feudal' tendencies developed merely from consciousness of 'Officer status', that led to the incident I am about to describe. In either event, the incident itself is both revealing and of some considerable general interest.

D. was keen on horse racing, though only in a very broad and ill-informed way, and went one Sunday to a small meeting in Germany sponsored and organized by the British Army of the Rhine, whose men and their horses were alone eligible to compete. It was thus an affair on the scale of a small point to point. The only betting was by means of a very amateur totalisator, which was run by members of the Royal Army Pay Corps and presided over by an elderly and plebeian Lieutenant-Colonel, himself also of the Pay Corps. Both the colonel and his men had given up their Sunday afternoon to do this, and though the Tote was hardly a triumph of speed or efficiency, it was, on the whole, remarkable as a piece of makeshift good will. To this Tote went Captain D. to bet on the last race of the afternoon. (He was of course in civilian clothes, but his status if not his identity was easily discernible in the closed circle of attendants.) Now the last race had only three runners, one of which, far superior in its record to the others, was owned and ridden by a well-known gentleman rider who was also, in the time he could spare, an officer of Hussars: this animal, it was thought with good reason, could only fail to win through the direct intervention of God. (It was called Satan's

Pride.) D., rightly surmising that the Tote dividend in case of such a looked-for victory would be minute, decided to back this favourite with a very substantial sum indeed, hoping that the sheer size of his wager would bring him a tangible return. It was also a good opportunity to show off, which he always enjoyed doing. Accordingly, on reaching the Tote, he demanded fifty pounds' worth of tickets on Satan's Pride. The corporal at the window went white and hurried off to fetch the colonel in charge, who appeared (since he was on duty of a kind) in a battered suit of battle dress, and took D. on one side. There was no reason, he said in broad Midland tones, why D. should not put £50 on a horse; but in this particular race everyone was backing Satan's Pride, the dividend, if it won, would in any case be negligible and D.'s £50 would make it almost non-existent—perhaps a penny-halfpenny in twenty shillings. Would D. consider lowering his stake and letting other people have a look-in? For D. must know that bets were normally very modest on this sort of occasion, and £50 was not only completely wrecking the market but was—well—rather ostentatious.

Instead of answering the old man in the courteous tones used to himself, D. completely lost control. With an occasional and insultingly stressed use of the word 'Sir', he demanded to know what an ex-ranker member of the Pay Corps, who came to a race meeting in uniform, could be expected to know about betting or gentlemen's habits in the matter, accused the colonel of snivelling, egalitarian, lower middle class prejudices, and finally shouted aloud that if Pay Corps officers were too mean or spineless to risk £50 on a horse, then it was time they had lessons from their betters. This D. would never have dared say if he also had been in uniform; and indeed it is remarkable that the Colonel did not ask his identity and report this intolerable conduct to our own C.O. As it was, the old man merely shrugged with good-humoured resignation and let D. have his way. I should add that Satan's Pride, having led by 200 yards, fell at the last fence, leaving Molly's Son to win and pay a dividend of ten pounds odd for a two-shilling ticket.

But the point is clear. Granted it was not very sensible of the colonel to interfere, however good his intentions, and granted much of D.'s outburst was due to thwarted exhibitionism and tax-free cognac: the plain fact remains that the incident was inspired by D.'s resentment that he, an officer, was being criticized by someone who did not, in a proper analysis, belong in the same category. The colonel, for a start, was in the Pay Corps, the officers of which could hardly aspire to the status of the Infantry; and in any case the old man simply was not a gentleman and, having emerged after years in the ranks, had no claim to possess the qualities with which D., trained as an officer from the beginning, must inevitably be blessed. This being the case, D. had ignored the entire official structure of the Army, not to mention the requirements of mere good manners, and given a blatantly feudal exhibition of hysterical spite. Nor is it insignificant that the colonel, at any rate from the immediate and practical point of view, would appear to have accepted the situation and let D. get away both with his insults and his demands.

If my reader will accept the validity of these brief sketches, he will see what I am getting at. The point is, not that these officers were cruel to their men or that, from a purely practical point of view, their various attitudes did not answer fairly well, but simply that they regarded themselves as so much set apart as to belong to a totally different class of human being—a class naturally designed to impose its will on all inferior classes.

But how, we must ask ourselves, did their painstaking educations at Sandhurst and Warminster achieve this unlooked-for and immoral result? My four examples were all middle class boys of desperately respectable, decent and dutiful families. There was no question of their having absorbed patrician ideas at their mothers' knee. Their families were not even military, so that neither was there any question of their having been reared in an atmosphere of cantonments and command. And yet here they were, plainly conscious that it was their absolute right to exercise unquestioned personal authority of this essentially feudal nature.

The answer lies in two fundamental elements of the education we have been at such pains to discuss. Firstly, the matter of segregation: secondly, and far more important, the insistence on the great quasi-moral imperatives. We have seen how a boy, selected as a potential officer at school, is set apart as such at his Regimental Depot. Now, this segregation is in itself merely the result of practical policy, and is intended to ensure that supposedly promising and intelligent boys enjoy more advanced and intensive training. But in fact the constant reference to the 'potential officers' squad', how it should do better than the others, how it is disgracing its name, how its members 'aren't officers yet'; the use of expressions like 'fine officers you'll make', 'behaviour not to be expected of . . .', 'by God, I'll give you officer'; all this, though only, I think, on a fairly superficial level, does prepare the ground very effectively for the sowing of the seed that is to grow into a blown and noxious sense of feudal superiority.

But the influence of the quasi-moral imperatives, our friends 'responsibility', etc., and the severe practical discipline based on these imperatives and undergone at Sandhurst, are the decisive factors. It all comes about this way. Boys chosen to be trained as officers are given no rest until they have absorbed certain moral influences 'which are essential to the character of an officer' and in themselves constitute a whole ethos. The transition from the imperative 'officers must have these qualities' to the general 'officers always do have these qualities' is easy. Then throw in the fact that these boys have always been set apart, both by their early education and in the Army, and it is equally easy to conclude that those so chosen must always, in a manner, have possessed these qualities and that training is merely designed to emphasize or bring them out. You have then passed, by two easy stages, from a state of affairs where certain, theoretically superior, qualities, are merely going to be taught, to a new conception whereby these very qualities are more or less conceded always to have existed in certain people—those chosen to become officers. Add to this the insistence on 'pride as an officer' ('an officer never falls out', etc., etc.) and you have completely deserted your original conception of officers being merely a highly trained professional body and have arrived at a notion of a moral *élite*—and, what is worse, at a notion of a natural or born moral *élite*. And there we have it. The right of command arrogated to themselves by officers is thus seen to be even more firmly based than the feudal right conferred by high birth on a landowning class; for this modern right of command is supposedly conferred by birth on a *morally* distinguished class and, thus conferred, is quite unquestionable by the average Englishman, the more so if he comes from those lower strata of the middle class which have always been so impressed by moral sanctions.

Before I conclude this essay, there are two further observations to be made—in themselves matter for an entire book. In the first place, once an officer is established, in his own view, as a member of a superior and order-giving class, he never loses his sense of superiority; but he can and often does lose all sense of the moral basis of this superiority and all the qualities which constitute this basis. He just becomes superior, as it were, *in vacuo*. He becomes a 'gentleman'. It is easy to see how the moral imperatives may lose their freshness when exposed to a dozen unfamiliar and exacting climates and a variety of retrograde influences—sexual opportunity, drink, the worldly air of worldly companions, or just sheer boredom. When this happens, one gets that product so typical of Britain—the amateur British officer. Highly trained professionally and morally, he has forgotten his professional techniques and sloughed his sense of moral obligation: but he has retained an unassailable sense of his own superiority (for is it not innate?) and absolute right to give orders. He still orders gin in the mess, possibly the only thing he ever does order, with the same God-given convictions as he would give a wrong order on the parade ground he so seldom visits. This may sound unpromising, but it brings about a situation in which perhaps we have something to be grateful for. In so far as the British officer regards his status as innate, he thinks of himself as a gentleman first and an officer second; it follows that professional jealousies, military caballing, 'juntaing', if you like, do not exist in the British Army to the extent that they can and do exist in armies whose officer corps are more self-consciously professional. British officers, on the one hand, do not constitute a militaristic menace; on the other hand, they are still sufficiently confident to rumble along and transact the Army's business quite adequately. From a practical point of view, this might seem a very reasonable solution to the problem of what sort of Army a democracy can tolerate. Our officers are not a danger to Government, just manage to get by, and eschew fanaticism. It is indeed an excellent solution; but only if you can accept the idea of increasing, year in, year out, the small but definite body of men who are convinced of their absolute and innate right to exercise the role of their class—command.

Secondly, it is important to note that the production and training of this new type of feudal officer—'neo-feudal', if you prefer—is the direct response of the military establishment to the demands of Hore Belisha and others after him that this same military establishment should change its ways and employ officers of professional rather than social qualifications. The Army got rid of Hore Belisha without much trouble, but these demands were constantly made throughout the war, and by 1945 it was obvious that the Socialist Government, backed by the country, was bent on deleting the last traces of social privilege from the military scene. Very well, replied the military establishment: we will accept boys of whatever class, provided they are sufficiently educated to undergo training, and we will ensure that the training itself contains liberal elements academically, and gives no advantage at all to the boy from the smart public school. But as we have seen in this essay, the regiments themselves have defiantly pursued their own policies in regard to the origins and incomes of the officers they accept; and, a matter of far greater significance, even boys of the least possibly feudal or privileged backgrounds, are being trained, by carefully inculcated moral influence, to regard themselves and their powers in exactly the same way as their predecessors—as Blimp, Marlborough, or even Richard the Lion Heart. Nor is there any reason to look for change. The Sandys reforms, popularly supposed to portend a more 'up to date' Army, are in fact concerned only to limit and reorganize those regiments whose functions are becoming obsolete and to introduce certain new and more technical emphases. In the course of all this, various regiments and officers will undoubtedly disappear, some of the more gilded regiments and officers among them. But this will only shrink the existing structure, it will not radically alter it. There will still be smart regiments with moneyed Etonians; and the other regiments, no matter how technical they may become, will still be officered by boys who, trained at Sandhurst as well as in scientific institutions, will still have absorbed sufficient military-cum-moral influences to arrogate to themselves the 'personal right to command' of which I have spoken in these pages. There is no way out. Whether you prefer a 'feudal' Etonian preening himself outside Buckingham Palace in a scarlet tunic, or a 'neo-feudalized' technician brimming with moral superiority in front of his rocket, is up to you. In the end they are both one and the same: whatever Hore Belisha may have said in 1939, however the nation may have opined in 1945, these are high quality establishment products—made to last.

So there it is. We have seen that an education of a basically moral nature convinces its recipients that they are an *élite*, so that to all intents they come to resemble a feudal class in their confirmed sense of status. Where I had expected to find a professional officer corps, I found a caste rooted in its own conception of superior, God-given status. It may be said we always knew this about the Army. I disagree. We always knew the Army had strict discipline, and in this sense some of us called it 'feudal'. We knew its officers tended to be snobbish, and in this sense again it was stigmatized as 'feudal'. But the current fashion in which the Army produces its caste of 'gentlemen', by convincing them that, whatever their social class, they were endowed at birth with unique qualities of character which entitle them to assume overlord status for all time, is a very different matter. For this was not the case before the war. At that time the appeal was directly aimed at purely social instincts of class superiority, not at the almost religious instincts that are worked upon today. It is the new generation, the men that have been coming out of Sandhurst since the war, that can most truly and clearly be seen to have perished by the Sword. They have perished in the sense that any man must perish who loses a proper notion of his place with and among other men. 'They are like pet animals': any man who can say this has, in a fashion, perished. The Sword, symbol of honour and leadership, kills in the back when it is also a symbol of caste. It lays waste its adherents and its enemies alike. For this sense of caste is a thing which cannot be shed. It eats into the soul like a cancer. Take heed, then, of the vampires, of the living dead who have perished by the Sword.

The Apotheosis of the Dilettante:

THE ESTABLISHMENT OF MANDARINS

by *Thomas Balogh*

Age 53. Economist. Fellow of Balliol College, Oxford, author of *The Dollar Crisis* and *Financial Organization*. Contributor to *Fabian International and Colonial Essays*.

I. The Victorian Reform

THE Victorians have come to be regarded as sanctimonious hypocrites, unable to face facts, fearful for their respectability, and therefore timid in action. In fact they ruthlessly destroyed the fabric of the feudal state and the prescriptive power of the aristocracy, ended the supremacy of the Church in the Universities and brought sceptical rationalism to triumph and, not the least, smashed the inefficiency of the old system of state administration based on corruption and nepotism. They conceived the role of the state in purely negative terms but were determined that those 'night-watchman' functions should be ably, efficiently and cheaply performed. There were to be no sinecures or spoils.

The Northcote-Trevelyan Report of 1854, whose centenary—as we shall see—was celebrated in so different a spirit from which it was conceived, was a model of bold innovation. It recommended the establishment of a unified Permanent Civil Service recruited by competitive examination. And against bitter resistance these principles were made fully effective by 1870; the Civil Service Commissioners 'to conduct tests' for 'the young men who may, from time to time be proposed to be appointed to junior situations in any of Her Majesty's Civil Establishments' having been established as early as May 1855. The reform of the Indian Civil Service had already been effected before that time.

Nor was the reform restricted to the narrow bureaucratic Establishment. The Victorians knew that they had to have a large *cadre* to fill the new posts adequately, and proceeded with equally ruthless determination to change completely the educational fabric of the country, starting with the so-called public schools, and not stopping at the archaic anomalies of the ancient universities. They knew what type of person and qualities they wanted: absence of corruption and favouritism on the one hand, and reticence from bureaucratic pretensions on the other. The negative virtues of state administration, the virtues which make life safe and agreeable for the strongest of private interests at home and in the Empire, were to be cultivated to the utmost.

It was an attitude of effortless superiority, combined with cultured scepticism, that was demanded from the Service (almost to the exclusion of others), and upon which that special mysterious art, Administrative Capacity, was said to depend. Positive knowledge and imagination, assertion of the social against the private interest, were obviously not looked for. The negative qualities were thought to be best attained by a judicious mixture of breeding, 'character-building' and a purposefully useless, somewhat dilettante, erudition which would keep 'dangerous thoughts' well away. All this could be best procured by selecting the cleverest from among an *élite* secure in its position and determined to defend it. Formal equality could be preserved yet effective choice limited mainly to the well-to-do, by demanding educational and social standards at the universities which ruled out the plebs—apart from a sprinkling of scholars—because of its high cost, without open discrimination: the rich and the poor were both to be permitted to dine at the Ritz.

A second essential ingredient, the cultivation of tolerant scepticism, was obtained by insisting on a formal kind of education, which developed powers of dialectical argument only, rather than a knowledge of the present world and its problems. Anything smacking of vocational training and technical knowledge was severely discountenanced. Classics or mathematics were the way of the chosen: in aristocratic Platonic philosophy and in the total demonstration of the futility of efforts at social betterment by ancient history, or in the formalism of mathematics, this was sought for. Finally, physical courage combined with complete intellectual conformity and an *esprit-de-corps* with an (mostly superficial) abnegation of self, was fostered through games, based on team-work rather than individual effort. Strict 'notions', and the tyranny of the prefect system which enforced unhesitating acceptance of rules evolved for the select (and stimulated contempt and disdain of everything outside the chosen circle) was thought to be a good basis for the maintenance of Empire. Hankering after the safety of tradition and precedent became the first and most characteristic of all traits of the public school product. The sausage-machine of Winchester provided perhaps the most typical of such products. Politicians and stock exchange pirates were better formed at Eton where the methods were, perhaps, different, though, it seems, not less efficient. The lesser schools tried to model themselves in one or the other direction, and compensated for lack of tradition by exaggerated compliance. This was, in my opinion, to be the origin of the undoing of the Empire it was supposed to uphold.[1]

This combination of Arnoldesque muscular Christianity with the basically unchanged feudal atmosphere of the old universities undoubtedly served the Victorians well (though perhaps not quite as well, after the late Victorian era of increasingly conscious technical education abroad, as many of its Oxbridge enthusiasts would have us believe). Family life in what American quasi-anthropologists would now call lower-upper or upper-middle class might have been happier with less inhibitions, but then Freud had not yet been invented, and such inconvenience as became increasingly noticeable, was put down to female 'vapours'. Within the limits of the Victorian social and economic framework, and so long as no positive duties devolved on the state, so long as it was sufficient to keep things basically as they were and not to interfere too much with 'other people's business', no obvious deficiency arose.

II. The fate of the Medlar

'The medlar gets rotten before its ripe'
Microcosmographia Academica, Cornford.

The most surprising fact about the British Civil Srevice is its novelty in its present structure. True, reform began over a hundred years ago. But it was not completed until after the First World War. Entry into the Civil Service no doubt has, since 1870, been pretty generally under the control of the Civil Service Commissioners; and the primacy of the Treasury was recognized as early

---

[1] A slight sense of unease has developed since I wrote this essay, even in impeccably respectable quarters. When *The Economist* (17 January, 1959, p. 196) is emboldened to write under the title 'How Green Are Our Diplomats?'
'Caught with their striped pants down in Baghdad, in Paris and now in Havana, Britain's diplomatic representatives need a closer examination than they themselves are evidently able to give to their surroundings.'
things have come to a pretty pass.

as 1867 'by giving its permanent head the title of Permanent Secretary and with a salary higher than that of other heads'.[1] Accounting Officers have been appointed by the Treasury since 1872. Yet until the First World War departmental autonomy was maintained and recruitment and promotion gave effective control to Ministers. The Lloyd George-Churchill combination effectively called in brilliant young men to build up the administrative structure needed by the reforms of 1906–12.[2] And the war was won by people recruited from all walks of life, especially from the universities. Prime Ministers and other important members of the Cabinet, prior to 1914, regularly employed private secretaries from outside the service, only dependent on the success of their masters. It was, on the whole, a small, compact, de-centralized service with little *positive* responsibility.

It was only after 1918 that the system of Civil Service organization planned by the Victorians became crystallized: a new corporation arose, vastly more important in the life of the nation than any other, while at the same time some of the safeguards wisely introduced by the Victorian reformers to avoid the creation of nepotistic privileged castes were surreptitiously weakened. As the bureaucracy grew stronger they grew bolder. Yet, by that time the problems and needs of the nation had completely altered, leaving it with an outdated and rather unsuitable bureaucratic organization. It became a vast, completely centralized service facing its ever-growing responsibilities with increasing insistence on a lack of expert knowledge. No Macaulay or Trevelyan arose to remedy this yawning insufficiency.

The establishment of a unitary Civil Service with vast powers was the result of the victory of the Treasury. A little after the end of the first war, Lloyd George, possibly because he had become far too dependent on the 'hard-faced' men whom he had called in to defeat the Whig-Asquithites, and possibly because he was really persuaded by Warren Fisher, then the Secretary of the Treasury, that these steps would make available the best talents of *all* departments for the new and thorny task of post-war reconstruc-

---

[1] Mackenzie and Grove, *Central Administration in Britain*, London 1957, p. 7. Much like the Pope's claims to Pepin's bequest, the Treasury also asserted that the Permanent Head was given the title Head of the Civil Service. The Minute was lost—like the earlier document but rather more surprisingly.

[2] Cf. below Mr. (subsequently Sir) R. C. K. Ensor's analysis.

tion, and thus secure promotion for all according to their deserts, decided to unify the service and to recognize the Permanent Secretary of the Treasury as Head of the Civil Service (Sept. 4, 1919).

From the point of view of the permanent bureaucrats this was total victory. The threat of outsiders, of Lloyd George's kindergarten (young men of great ability and expertise advising him directly—a method, as we shall presently see, was his way of bypassing bureaucratic obstacles in the way of winning the war) was to be eliminated once and for all.

This ruling was followed up by a further ukase laying down that the consent of the Prime Minister would be required to any vital appointment in *all* departments. This included the permanent heads, their deputies and their principal finance and establishment officers in their turn controlling departmental promotions. The Prime Minister of course would have practically no knowledge of the intricate personal equations and objective needs concerned or of the real qualities of the potential candidates, and would be advised by the Head of the Civil Service. The departmental Minister retained the right not of proposal but merely of veto.

The power-equation between the bureaucracy and the elected political representatives of the governed was in this way drastically changed.[1] The departmental Minister was, of necessity, in the main a non-expert. He was, moreover, in most cases 'non-permanent' in the literal, and not merely in the political, sense of the word. A tenure of three years of a single office by a Minister is the exception not the rule. (Mr. Lennox-Boyd is perhaps the only exception in modern political experience.) His knowledge of people in his Department must, therefore, of necessity be limited, and of other Civil Service candidates to the chief posts in his Department, even less. Repeated demands for change in these

[1] At the formation of the first post-war Conservative Government, Mr. Lyttelton (now Lord Chandos) was strongly tipped for the post of Chancellor. In the event Mr. Butler was appointed. Sir Edward Bridges visited Sir Winston Churchill before the nomination was announced. One cannot help wondering whether the Head of the Civil Service performed the role claimed for the Sovereign by his official biographer in the case of the sudden switch of Dr. Dalton and Mr. Bevin—though not confirmed by Mr. (now Lord) Attlee. (*King George VI* by Sir J. W. Wheeler Bennett. London 1958, pp. 638–9.) If so, the real equilibrium in the state seems to have shifted even further than is feared by pessimists. Like the Pretorian Guard, the Civil Service might now be in a position at least to veto inconvenient or unconventional appointments.

appointments, however justified they may be, have not been popular with any of the Prime Ministers who have recently been in office—least of all Mr. (now Lord) Attlee (perhaps Mr. Macmillan has been less 'respectable' and timid in this respect than any other chief minister).

In the event, the influence of the Treasury became paramount throughout the Service through the new system of promotion. Thus a tight new caste of mandarins has come to be created as the crowning of the Victorian reforms. No longer were officials dependent for the highest prizes in their careers on their success within their Departments, as was the case when these were almost independent in their policy of promotion, which encouraged a spirit of reform. Constructive thinking became a dangerous quality. It was 'reputation for solid commonsense' i.e. the favour of a small Treasury clique, which became decisive. The fact that Civil Servants are supposed to be permanent has, far from promoting detailed and free thought, resulted in a depressing conformity—very different from earlier periods.

The movement to uniformity and towards the crystallization of the Victorian principle of 'effortless superiority'—in other words lack of special knowledge—culminated by the establishment in 1921 by an Order-in-Council of 'Treasury' classes, in the first instance of so-called 'general' classes, in the Civil Service. Departmental individuality received its final quietus. Together with the effective predominance of the Treasury, this measure formally established the superiority of those recruits to the Civil Service who had no professional or technical qualifications.[1]

The technical classes of specialists were created subsequently

---

[1] Of these only the Administrative Class has any importance from the point of view of policy-making.

The mobility from the lower to higher classes has increased. Sir Horace Wilson was himself a promoted executive officer and several departmental heads have risen from the ranks. This does not mean that the spirit of the highest Civil Servants has changed. The promoted warrant officers and privates have mostly outdone each other in imitating the worst characteristics of the public school educated graduates of the old universities, just as the angry young men are railing against the Welfare State which enabled them to become coherently vocal. One of the oddest manifestations of this spirit is an attack by a 'Young Executive Officer' in the *Civil Service Opinion* (Jan. 1958) on the ills of the Service. Not a word is said about the need for knowledge and technical training. The plea is for 'straight line' promotion, i.e. apparently for the creation of mandarins without even the need for university training or examination but with aptitude for 'leadership', whatever that may mean.

and their status and pay is a reflection of their relative inferiority to the 'general administrator'. In the main, promotion to the higher ranks is reserved for the latter, though the 'specialist', at the cost of having to shelve his special knowledge, can be 're-classified', and enter the stream of general promotion. Yet there can be no doubt of the excellence of these 'technical' services.

At the very moment when the victory first of manhood, and subsequently of universal, suffrage changed the whole fabric of Government, and the majestic powers of a modern state began to be used to counteract the ferocious rush of 'free' market economies towards inequality and insecurity, the instrument by which this universal demand of democratic politics had to be accomplished was fossilized into an inert obstacle. The principle that administrators must be willing and able to do any work seems to have been interpreted so as to waste accumulated technical knowledge more and more by rapid variation of assignments. This practice had to have devastating effects all down the line but was exaggerated in the highest levels. In some departments, e.g. foreign affairs, colonies, and at home, the planning of economic policy, it was obviously more in evidence, by continued and manifest failure of intelligence and policy, than elsewhere.

In fields in which specialized knowledge or training is required to carry on a sustained argument, the absence of such specialized knowledge invariably leads – not to the absence of theorizing, to 'hard-headed realistic empiricism' – but to jejeune meditations based on a set of simple theology and beliefs, if not on some long-since exploded fallacy. If expert knowledge is unavailable all along the line or (what is more probable) carefully hidden by any junior official in fear of his career, these defects could only be detected by a Minister. But Ministers themselves are dilettantes. From the decision to elevate the general administrator, the mandarin, and grant to his corporation supreme influence, much of the present discomfiture of the country has followed. Hardly ever has so anachronistic a change occurred in a vital organ of a great empire at a worse moment. The discrepancy between tasks and means is still steadily increasing.

Nor was that all. With the rapid increase in the duties of the State dictated by modern democratic politics, duties which prove complex administrative problems, a vast expansion of the Service has taken place. The non-industrial Service grew from

116,713 in 1901 to 280,900 in 1914. By 1939 it reached the level of 387,400 and expanded to a maximum of 710,600 in 1943. In 1955 it was still 625,436, i.e. still almost double the pre-war figure and only about 10 per cent below the wartime peak.[1] The expansion of some key departments dealing with the nation's economic destiny, and especially of the policy-making element was even more startling.[2] A more violent expansion of numbers (not to say functions) can hardly be imagined.

In stark contrast to this dynamism is the immobility of the structure, not merely of the general but also of the departmental organization. As of old, when a handful of gentlemen decided on those few policy questions in which the State was thought to have a legitimate say (and in which Ministers and Members of Parliament had equal if not greater competence), these vast masses of highly gifted men are still managed by a handful of Permanent Secretaries, and their deputies, through whom *all* important business has to be transacted. The collegiate system which has prevailed over the Presidential constitution even in American public life and private business organization, and which has always dominated British public life, has found no impact in the Service. The office of the Lord High Admiral or Treasurer, of the Commander in Chief, have all been put 'into Commission' as the duties, the patronage and therefore the power, concentrated in the hands of the holder threatened to become overwhelming. The power of the Head of the Civil Service, through the patronage he wields, is far beyond the wildest dreams of the territorial oligarchs of the eighteenth century. It has been further increased

---

[1] Mackenzie and Grove, op. cit., pp. 7 and 22.

[2] *The Organisation of the British Central Government 1914–1956.* Ed. D. N. Chester, written by F. M. G. Willson. London 1957, pp. 52, 92, 120, 130, 146, 163, 183, 194.

The increases in non-industrial staffs in the key departments was startling:

	1914	1935	1956
Financial Departments	20,365	37,765	69,520
Of which Treasury	125	250	1,260
Trade and Industry	7,720	33,045	64,705
P.O.	208,890	165,890	252,940
Law, Justice and Public Order	7,120	11,535	18,965
Social Services Depts.	5,515	18,885	60,740
Foreign Affairs	980	2,380	8,420

It is interesting to note that the expansion in the Treasury was almost as vigorous as in any other Department: personnel rose roughly tenfold.

by the growth in the number of important posts in nationalized industries and other public boards which have to be filled. But the Heads of other departments too are confronted with such a load of tasks and wield such power that earlier and more realistic generations of political leaders and, of course, all prudent private organizations would long have put them into commission.

Two further developments took place also more recently. The first was a change in the system of recruitment. The second, the change in the relation of the Civil Service personnel to the outside world.

Already before the last war, in connection with the broadening of the syllabus of the competitive examination (and possibly to counteract the consequences of the increasing democratization of education, the change in the social background of many potentially successful competitors, in consequence of the improvement of higher popular education after the 1902 and 1914 Education Acts), greater weight was given to the interview. Thus the safeguards against class-prejudice and nepotism established by the anonymity of the written examination were considerably weakened.

The selectors were selected and non-conformists were obviously not chosen. Old civil servants and other representatives of the Establishment were in a safe majority. After the Second World War the Civil Service used the opportunity presented by the existence of a complacent Labour Government to go much further in this direction. The theory was insidiously plausible. A new 'modern' method of psychological testing (the so-called country-house system) was adopted which would bring out those important requirements of a successful performance of the duties of a Civil Servant that cannot be tested by an examination of intellectual excellence. A qualifying examination would safeguard the Service against blatant abuse. And a serious interview would bring Civil Service, university and common sense experience to bear on the selection of young entrants. General qualities of intelligence and leadership and not merely educational advantage (in England said to be largely connected with social background) would—so the theory went—come into its own. It all sounded most progressive. So tempting, indeed, seemed the prospect that Mr. Bevin was brought to accept it as the sole way of recruitment to the Foreign Service. It is said—perhaps maliciously—that he expected to be able in this way to leaven the entry into the Office by some young trade unionist hopefuls.

What in fact has happened is that the qualifying examination is too weak to exclude feeble intellects. The rather stiffer—but in itself quite inadequate—intellectual requirement that the candidate must have gained second-class honours at a university, can be easily evaded by permitting the acceptance by the Civil Service Commissioners of a certificate of the teachers of the candidate that he was to all intents and purposes eligible because his failure to obtain the required degree was due to some special circumstances. The test itself, so far as one can make out from a long experience with pupils taking it, seems to favour the grasshopper mind and the exhibitionist. So far from being a psychological test, psychologists are in a small minority on the committee. But whatever the merits or demerits of the 'test' (and it has, in its time, given rise to passionate feelings expressed mainly in letters to *The Times*, the Tories attacking and Labour defending the new method because it sounded un-English and odd to the one, and progressive to the other), what is striking is that it has little influence. The interview is so heavily weighed in the end-result that the effective choice—complete morons barred—is made by the interviewing board on which prejudice is only too well represented (though there are always a suitably small number of progressive dons and other outsiders present). A new type of favouritism, if not nepotism, has been obviously infiltrating into the system.[1]

If the study of the social sciences, and in particular of economics and statistics has been admitted as an avenue into the Service, there has been no effort to stimulate such studies among potential candidates—if long years' experience as tutor in an Oxford College which is usually well represented among the successful entrants might be quoted; there seems a tendency among economic departments and especially the Treasury to favour—other things being equal—people without economic education. The reason for this is not far to seek—especially not for those who read Professor Parkinson.

Nor is there any attempt at serious training. The young administrator is given some 'notions' or indoctrination on the fashionable views held by important departments without being

[1] The continued failures of the Foreign Office are not unconnected with this development (cf. below).

encouraged to question their rationale. Despite the recommendation of various Committees there has been no effort at any basic
vocational preparation in the essential intellectual techniques
needed to sort out British social and economic problems. The
French Higher School of Administration is a good example of
such an effort at fitting candidates for their job. Nor is there beyond
the secondment mainly of economists to Universities and International Agencies (to which reference will be made below) any
effort to have refresher courses analogous to the Staff College in
the Fighting Services. Together with the predominance of
classics and mathematics, this necessarily encourages acceptance
of precedents, however ill-fitting, and a refusal, because of incapacity, to think out problems afresh. Timid beginnings to change
are usually ended by some economy drive or another. Educational
efforts can hardly show any immediate effects. They are likely
victims of any demagogic clamour for cutting State extravagance
and reducing taxation.

The second change has been subtler but not less important.
It is the consequence of the growing importance of State activities
in the sum total of the national product, as consumers of the
products of private industry, as regulators of private productive
activity, and with the increased share of collectively owned or
run enterprise (the patronage of which is to a large extent[1] in
their hand), the relationship of the Civil Servant to private
industry has completely changed.

I shall deal with the resultant consequences on the requirements of policy making, the need for a *positive* attitude, presently.
In this context a different, and rather delicate problem has to be
dealt with. This is the problem of the growing inter-change of
personnel between Civil Service and private firms, or rather the
tendency of Civil Servants to play an increasingly important role
in business.[2] Now there has always been such inter-change, and

---

[1] Much more under a Labour Government than under the Tories. The
extreme sensitivity of the Labour leaders to accusations of jobbery contrasts
sharply with the complacent patronage of the retired Civil Servant and the
confident knowledge of the Tories that government *means* 'jobs for the boys'.
Labour never succeeded in building up a Progressive Establishment. Even
Liberals were better at this vital task. I shall return to this theme presently.

[2] A related problem is the use of posts in nationally-owned companies for
retirement 'perks' or work for people who have to be got rid of. Much of the
discontent with nationalized industries (including the Suez Canal and the

distinguished Civil Servants and Pro-Consuls—Imperial or
Diplomatic—after their retirement, generally at a relatively
young age (but seldom before they were due to retire), have
always tended to accept jobs with private merchant firms, banks
and even industries. With increasing average age and taxation,
the need to obtain such jobs obviously increases. The opportunity
of obtaining them has also obviously increased with the vastly
increased duties, and powers, of Civil Servants. And the differences
in remuneration have not diminished, especially if due and
realistic account is taken of the 'perks' of private employment in
the shape of expense accounts, 'top hat' pension schemes, and
other contributions of one kind or another.

Now in the past, apart from exceptional circumstances which
mainly arose in the Empire, the employment by private firms of
Civil Servants could be of little *direct* advantage to anyone, i.e.
due to the personal influence of the Civil Servant with his late
colleagues, because the powers of the State were rather limited.
In the altered circumstances of the managed Welfare State—
Labour or Tory—this has completely changed. State policy
decisions have become more vitally important and the decision
can easily be influenced one way or another by judicious summing
up.

Of course the British Civil Service is not subject to direct
corruption (though there were and are more exceptions to this
rule than most would admit—especially in the Colonial Empire).
The formal position is quite clear:[1]

'To say that (a Civil Servant) is not to subordinate his duty
to his private interest, nor to make use of his official position to
further those interests is to say no more than he must behave
with common honesty. The Service exacts from itself a higher
standard, because it recognizes that the State is entitled to

[1] Mackenzie & Grove, *op. cit.* 151–2.

British Petroleum Company the majority of whose shares was in public hands)
can be traced to this pernicious practice and the timidity of the Labour Ministers
of 1945–51. Until Labour evolves a satisfactory way of recruitment into the
nationalized industry, the present discontents are unlikely to disappear. Yet,
even now, the dispute of the two wings of the Party is about what to nationalize
and not how to run the industry once it has been nationalized.

demand that its servants shall not only be honest in fact but beyond the reach of the suspicion of dishonesty.'

and

'Much of our policy in regard to taxation, industrial controls, Government contracts, social services, is only possible because there is complete confidence that the officials (whatever their other human failings) are not lining their own pockets at the public's expense, and are not acting so as to favour one interest at the expense of another. The principle extends from great matters to very small ones. A high official must not discuss with a business magnate the possibility of a job after retirement, if the magnate's business is in any way the concern of the official's department; nor may he accept such a post before two years after his retirement unless he obtains the permission of his former Minister and the Treasury.'

No doubt the Civil Service work hard and give what is according to their lights disinterested advice and are not blatant in job-hunting. But is this enough? How, in particular, should one define the 'concern of a Department'? What higher official in what major Department could be of *no direct* use to a large firm?[1] Can one agree fully with the two distinguished authors of the latest analysis of the *Central Administration of Britain* when they say:[2]

'Few cases (of professional intermediaries) were found, and some of these were fraudulent, in that payment was claimed for influence not really exercised. Others were genuine cases of former members of Departments who were able to sell useful experience of the regulations; an embarrassing development, not unlike the appearance of income tax inspectors as tax accountants. The British have great faith in "a man who knows a man who knows a man who . . . ", in the strength of the "old boy network". Undoubtedly there are some large private

---

[1] As I do not intend to make any specific aspersions against anybody I had to change my example twice in the six months since I first penned this sentence: so many of the most unlikely combinations, chosen because they seemed unlikely, have come to pass.

[2] *Ibid.* p. 453.

concerns which have, through personal relationships, particularly good lines of entry to the ministries on which they depend, but this often arises out of an inter-locking between a Department and the firms which serve it, which is convenient to both parties, and perhaps also operates in the public interest by facilitating an easy exchange of ideas.'

And it is not at least blindly complacent to say:[1]

'A firm which recruits a distinguished administrative or technical Civil Servant gains a proved man trained for it by the government. Government gains in that it has placed its own man in a key position.'

What can the phrase 'its own man' possibly signify in this context?

Finally, it is not the threat of unfairness as between one private firm and another that is really at issue. What is at issue is not that particular *douceur* will result in particular compliance.[2] What is far, far more important is the reaction of those men (or at least of the general average of those men), who remain in the Service, who will also wish to do well and will therefore be—in most cases quite unconsciously—inclined to take a general view of things not awkward to large private interests. After all radical troublemakers are seldom asked to accept directorships. Here again adherence to old, merely negative Victorian safeguards, is no longer enough.

III. Fact and Fancy

THE period before and since 1954, the centenary of the great Northcote Trevelyan Report, saw the publication of innumerable books, pamphlets and articles[3] celebrating the foundations, and extolling the virtues of the British Civil Service. In a spirit very

---

[1] *Ibid.* It is not the tax inspector who should arouse embarrassment but much higher candidates.

[2] The inquiry about the alleged 'leak' of the Bank rate showed the appalling consequences on the quality of policy-making of this ubiquitous 'old boy' net: but the financial consequences of any irregularities would have been trivial— if there had been any irregularities.

[3] And novels, such as Sir Charles Snow's panegyrics on the wisdom of the conformists. The uncritical nature of most of these publications can be explained by the fact that they were written by Civil Servants on active service—and more

different from that of Macaulay or Trevelyan, the anniversary of that event has been dedicated to show that the organization then conceived for a wholly different task and unchanged in all fundamental respects, was still functioning with matchless perfection. No hint is given that new qualities are needed for the problems of the present era of revolutionary political and economic change, and the increasing risk of oligarchic domination of political and economic life by large-scale organizations, or those consequent to the establishment of a Welfare State and to the government undertaking the positive duty of providing employment while preserving stability.

The picture emerges of the Civil Service machine adapting itself smoothly to the will of Ministers, whatever the Party in power, and however abrupt the change in outlook after elections. The Ministers initiate policy (needing detailed expert knowledge) and respond pliably to the democratic control of Parliament. Is question-time in the House of Commons not the essence of the British way of political life, to which all distinguished foreign visitors are invited to pay due homage? Does not Mr. (now Earl) Attlee—whose overwhelming mandate for radical reform in 1945 was (unlike the Liberal landslide of 1906) wasted away in four exchange crises and mounting prices—hurry and testify:[1]

'I do not think that this remarkable attribute of impartiality in the British Civil Service is sufficiently well known or adequately recognized for what it is—one of the strongest bulwarks of democracy, and I am often at pains to point this out';

and

[1] Robson, *op. cit.* p. 16 and p. 24. One almost suspects that Mr. (now Lord) Attlee was trying to parody the persiflage of his own autobiography by Mr. Christopher Hollis in *Punch*.

especially by a small selected group around Sir Edward (now Lord) Bridges, the head who controlled the machine. This is true of the Whitehall Series as well as Prof. Robson's compendium on *The Civil Service in Britain and France*, (Hogarth Press). But this fact is itself rather surprising and needs explanation. Nor has there been any really serious effort at sociological analysis by outsiders. Both Prof. Mackenzie's and Prof. S. Beer's book (*Treasury Control*) represent an uncritical exposition of the official line. The latter celebrated the perfection of Treasury Control a few months before. Mr. Macmillan complained about out-dated Bradshaws and completely reorganized the higher echelons of the office. A more eloquent comment is not needed.

'The Civil Servant forms part of a service unequalled in all the world—one of the causes of just pride in his fellow-countrymen'.

Nor do his late colleagues take a more critical line in the same book. There is no hint in most learned academic contributions[1] that there is anything amiss in the existing structure of British Administration, in the relations of Ministers to their advisers, and in the system of recruitment and promotion of the latter.

Yet it is not difficult to show that the image of a smoothly and efficiently working parliamentary democracy is one of the most extravagant of all British myths. Its rise has to a large extent been due to the vanity of the politicians and the genius at public relations of the heads of our bureaucracy. Successful salesmanship has always been regarded as a particularly American accomplishment. It was Col. Lee, after all, who started it. It was he who transformed the senior Rockefeller's public face into a paragon of forward looking economic statesmanship and piously benign benefaction. Yet he and the ever-growing number of public-relation geniuses in Madison Avenue—not to forget San Francisco—who now sell Presidents, Vice-Presidents and costly and inefficient medical services or other conservative policies cellophane-packed to the unsuspecting American televiewing public look piteously amateurish when compared with the accomplishments of Sir Edward (now Lord) Bridges and his colleagues. Those glossy American campaigns have, after all, to be paid for in hard cash. And the initiated know what to make of them.

Not so our Civil Service. They do not have to hire expensive copywriters, they do the job themselves, ably helped by their own victims—the politicians. Effective power without responsibility, the complete freedom from all criticism, and last but not least, the attainment of higher salaries than their Ministerial chiefs[2]—

[1] Prof. Beer's book is typical in this respect. In his narrative post-war British difficulties in economic policy-making ended in 1947 when the Treasury, under Sir Stafford Cripps, took charge of economic planning. Not a word is said of the 1949 crisis leading to the devaluation of the pound or of the 1951 crisis leading to the fall of Labour. Complete silence is preserved about the checkered financial history since 1952.

[2] The Priestley Report on the Higher Civil Service (signed by the most eloquent of all protagonists for greater equality in the wage structure, Lady Wootton) not merely fails to impose strict prohibition on the acceptance of jobs in private business; not only assigns a higher salary to Permanent Secretaries than even Cabinet Ministers receive but sharply reverses the narrowing of

such are the rich rewards of their skilful efforts. And the new myth created, not equalled since the divine right of kings, has found ready acceptance in the most select academic circles dedicated to a searching analysis of the essence of political relations.

Now myths can be useful, indeed indispensable. They can energize people to efforts not otherwise attainable. They must not be condemned out of hand. There are, however, fatal myths. They serve to blind people to their problems and in their complacency destroy all hopes of solving them. Given the frightful dangers to which Britain is exposed economically as well as politically, and the need to preserve Britain's international influence, such myths must be ruthlessly exposed.

Now there can be little doubt that the myth of a perfectly working Government machine, just as the mystique created round the concept of the new Commonwealth, belongs to this category. Britain's power has been declining at a rate unparalleled since the crash of the Spanish Empire, and the decline cannot be explained by the venality of the voters, or the folly of politicians acting in a democratic system, or even the harshness of the world. The fact alone that Britain was struck by five severe exchange crises since the war, and still has not solved its basic problems of reconciling growth and stability, that it could not satisfactorily solve the problems of running nationally owned enterprise, would not by itself necessitate a review of the policy-making machinery. The problems facing Britain after the war, it must be admitted, were exceptional.

What makes a review of the policy-making machinery imperative is that all these acute crises and this creeping paralysis share in having taken the authorities unawares, though they were predictable and predicted by the critics of the policy pursued. They all left Britain relatively and even absolutely weaker; yet the impact of the war and of the revolutionary changes in international economic and political relations all demand increased strength for increased effort. The fact is that in internal administration, and policy and external relations, Ministers of both parties had no

---

differentials achieved since the outbreak of the war. This was further enhanced by the permanent committee that has been created to safeguard the interests of the Higher Civil Service.

chance of mastering the growing troubles as they were at best not supplied with all the facts, and at worst supplied with misleading appreciations.

Mr. Chamberlain or Mr. Baldwin perhaps could hardly be excused for the unnecessary drift towards war and catastrophe. But in all fairness it should be pointed out that their official Treasury advisers not merely gave a completely false picture of the magnitude of the Nazi rearmament effort[1] but also predicted with confidence that the strain caused would end in an effortless elimination of the dictators by bankruptcy.

Has our intelligence service, foreign and domestic, and our policy-making improved since? Can we really pretend that all was well with the expert knowledge on the basis of which post-war Middle Eastern or German policy was made? How was it possible to be regularly caught unawares by developments in Jordan or Iraq, by the revolutions in Havana and South America. How did it come about that our appreciation of the relative fighting capabilities of the Jews was as faulty as that of President Nasser, and that both the theoretical and the political intelligence about the prospects of our plans—the Free Trade Area proposal—for our relations with Europe, and especially about the likely strength of the Franco-German Axis opposing them were hopelessly inaccurate.[2] There has been a tragic monotony of failure to appreciate the meaning of changes, social and political, to measure the strength of nascent national feeling, to gauge the impact on Britain, to devise policies to strengthen the country's diplomatic, political and economic strength to cope with it.

The result is the weakening of the links of the Commonwealth, the loss of allegiance of peoples in British colonies and spheres of influence which could easily have been secured by a less exclusive,

---

[1] In 1938 an estimate I made of the Nazi rearmament (which turned out, on the basis of the data captured at the end of the war to be some 25 per cent too low) was said by the two Treasury experts in charge of German economic intelligence to be about 100 per cent too high. Yet even after May 1940 no effort was made to rectify the method of estimate.

[2] The Suez episode must be strictly excluded from this list of failures. It was, from the beginning to the end, a 'democratic' ministerial venture approved by the large unintelligent majority of the nation. That also is a fact serious enough to take proper note of. Its dismal stupidity and inevitable failure does not make Glubb's or Kirkbride's efforts less astonishingly and disastrously irrelevant to modern policy-making.

less arrogantly (and unjustifiably) superior attitude by Britain's representatives.[1] How much of British influence and power could have been saved in the Middle-East, in Africa and Asia by a little more tact, a little more imagination and (admittedly a lot more) expert knowledge.[2] As it was, a passionate desire for independence from all things British was first evoked by official policy, followed by denials that anything was amiss except the murderous wildness of a few agitators. This was followed by riots, arrests, prescriptions and, soon after, by bloodshed, and ended by having to make far more extreme concessions than would have sufficed in the beginning, to the detriment of both British influence, and native prosperity.

There might no doubt exist a certain number of Departments where pure intelligence, not modified by theoretical knowledge and factual experience, might suffice. I do not know whether the Ministry of Works or Pensions are cases in point—though some unflattering evidence seems to have emerged in regard to the latter in recent debates on National Superannuation. The Ministry of Health has been sharply condemned by the official historian of social services during the war for its callous attitude before the war.[3] The failure to rise fully to the vast opportunity in efficiently and imaginatively organizing the Health Service, one of Britain's unique contributions to Social Welfare, has more recently been

[1] I have had something to do with the negotiations on Malta's integration into the U.K. and can testify on these basic reasons of the failure of this imaginative concept of Mr. Mintoff. The volatile changeability of the Service Chiefs in their appreciation of Malta's strategic role was as surprising as the complete incapacity of the Colonial Office to produce experts capable of discussing seriously Mr. Mintoff's social and economic proposals. The result was that he was confronted with brusque ultimata on his demands for British help instead of detailed and reasoned counter-proposals. The Treasury then took over, blindly slashing estimates and unable to safeguard its own interests in economy. Such was their ignorance that their choice of experts proved their own undoing. The retired Civil Servants sent out to Malta usually granted more to Mr. Mintoff in wages and subsidies than he originally demanded, and complicated his efforts to carry through a coherent programme of reconstruction. In the end their ham-handed dealing with the problem of the dockyard drove Mr. Mintoff —accustomed as he had become to oriental bargaining by the British—into unreasonable counter-attitudes which caused the final break.

[2] Cf. below.

[3] Prof. Titmuss, *Problems of Social Policy*, pp. 120–125 and p. 514, footnote 2.

equally sharply criticized in the Acton Society's Report,[1] the authors of which included Sir George Schuster. As *The Times* summed up the argument: 'The Ministry will not be equipped to do its task properly until it is substantially staffed with men with ripe experience in managing and developing hospital health services.'

On how many other fields does this judgment hold with equal or greater force? I have no doubt that in the vital field of foreign and colonial affairs it has been completely established in the last decades. It is even perhaps more apt so far as economic policy-making is concerned, to which I now turn.

IV. The Machinery for economic policy-making

The problem of economic policy-making is admittedly extremely difficult. Economics is not an exact science if it is a science at all and not a kind of art. Economic issues are very rarely free of political and social implications and administrative problems which often dominate the choice of a solution. As Sidgwick wrote, however, in the introduction to his *Principles of Political Economy* (p. 14):[2]

'It is very rarely, if ever, that the practical economic questions which are presented to the statesman can be unhesitatingly decided by abstract reasoning from elementary principles. For the right solution of them full and exact knowledge of the facts of a particular case is commonly required; and the difficulty of ascertaining these facts is often such as to prevent the attainment of positive conclusions by any strictly scientific procedure.

'At the same time, the function of economic theory in relation to such problems is none the less important and indispensable; since the practical conclusions of the most

[1] When I first wrote this passage it read "It is just conceivable that hospital management is better done by people not involved in sectional quarrels (though one might presume that someone steeled by, and having risen above, the melée might be preferable even there)."

[2] I owe the quotation and some of the ideas to Mr. D. Henderson of Lincoln College, Oxford.

untheoretical expert are always reached implicitly or explicitly by some kind of reasoning from some economic principles; and if the principles or reasoning be unsound the conclusions can only be right by accident.'

Thus a lack of competent and well-trained economists would have serious implications on our prospects at a juncture when British relative strength is ebbing away and needs utmost efforts for its reinforcements. As I have already pointed out the absence of training does not make for the absence of 'theory'. It usually results in a bias towards a policy of 'do-nothing' in the fond—and jejune—hope that a negative absolves them from any positive responsibility.

The importance of economic policy-making is enhanced by the fact that eventually all proposals involving spending will come under the baleful eye of the Treasury, whose traditional role (as the Department responsible for the preparation of estimates of 'Supply') is to oppose any increase in expenditure. Thus instead of a coherent co-ordination of policy there is some danger of a series of partial engagements between the Treasury and each separate spending Department. This danger is enhanced by the consequences of the system of Cabinet responsibility and administrative procedure. In the absence of a considered long-term plan, co-ordination must be through *ad hoc* or permanent interdepartmental committees in the first instance on the official level. These committees resemble peace conferences between sovereign powers at which representatives of the several Departments keep strictly to their briefs which of necessity represent pleas for their 'own' vested interests, rather than an objective review of the case from a national standpoint. In the ensuing bargain there is—again of necessity—no guarantee that an 'impartial' member with economic competence will insist on due regard to that standpoint. The Treasury will have its own vested interest, i.e. a cut in expenditure above all in view, and, among its staff, men with even elementary knowledge of economics are the rare exception rather than the rule. Of the top score of officials only one, the Head of the Economic Section, is an economist. Thus technical knowledge in this supremely important field is not unlikely to make its due contribution only by—rare—accident.

It should be emphasized that the present position represents a substantial advance over the pre-war system. After Lloyd George's attempts to bring in outside experts there was in the Treasury no patience with economists. Mr. (now Sir Ralph) Hawtry, was isolated in his theoretical studies and without influence (except when he was needed to buttress the prejudice of his chiefs by appropriate argument, as in the case of the so-called 'Treasury-principle' which flatly denied the efficacy of Government spending to increase employment). The so-called Economic Adviser to the Government—no economist—was (like the Diplomatic Adviser) powerless.

The wartime organization of an Economic Section at the Cabinet Office (which grew out of a more informal committee of economists) was not completely undone after the victory of 'freedom'. The Central Statistical Office, which was hived off already during the war, was left in the Cabinet Office. The Economic Section was put into the Treasury. It has always commanded and still commands the service of experts of great renown. Unfortunately it is, on crucial occasions,[1] not consulted and the paucity of its staff often prevents it from making its influence felt at lower levels, before a question comes up for final decision. In other Departments there are no economists, as such, in a position to advise Ministers. If, then, even short term decisions are often taken without due expert knowledge, there is little if any possibility at all for long term planning. This woeful shortage of economic insight does not—even under a Labour Government, pledged to economic planning—seem to have been as much as realized.

A successful scheme of temporary appointment in the Economic Section has been initiated for younger economists for one or two years at a time. This scheme is admirable. The Treasury has, moreover, consented from time to time to give leave of absence to established Civil Servants with a bent and liking for academic research to spend one or two years at the universities; a scheme which has also benefited both sides. They can hardly be commended too highly. But such schemes cannot serve as substitutes for the increasing use of experts in the regular Civil Service. In that respect the situation has steadily worsened of late. Up to the absorption of the Economic Section of the Cabinet

---

[1] This is clear from the evidence of Sir Roger Makins before the 'Leak' Tribunal (esp. Questions 10587–10627).

Offices into the Treasury recruits into that section could secure establishment in the Civil Service at least as economists and secure hearing. Thus a way was open to enlist economic experts into the permanent establishment of the Civil Service, though they still had to be re-classified in order to become eligible for promotion in the general service. This apparently has now ceased. In consequence, the Economic Section, excellent service though it has tried to render, has been deprived of very able men who saw no hope of making a career. Such economists moreover as happened to have been recruited through the ordinary examinations were not employed on problems of economic policy. Their accumulated knowledge, so precious for the country, runs to waste.

The consequences are there for all to see. The disastrous effects of the Treasury's and the Bank of England's financial policy during the inter-war period are no longer questioned.[1] They left Britain economically weaker and its population shocked by the traumatic experience of mass-unemployment.

The impact of the Treasury during the Second War was almost fatal. At its beginning the successful opposition of the Treasury and the Bank of England against a firm control of foreign payments cost the country hundreds of millions in gold. Fortunately President Roosevelt's Lend-Lease scheme came to the rescue. But given the strength of the American isolationist sentiment, the weakening of our foreign exchange reserves might have meant the difference between life and death.

After the battle I had waged, with the full support of Lord Keynes,[2] for effective exchange of control was over in June 1940,

[1] Though the official History of War-time Financial Policy manages without conscious irony to describe the main author of the return to the pre-war gold parity as a man "whose keen interest in the reconstruction of British industry had already shown itself in many ways during the inter-war period" (p. 139).

[2] Subsequently (and in sharp contrast with Hubert Henderson) he succumbed to the influence of the Treasury and the *laissez-faire* economists attached to it and went to his death through the bitter disappointment of the Savannah Conference. It is interesting to note that both in the First and Second World Wars Keynes showed complete inability to grasp the *physical* planning aspect of the war economic problem. He was much responsible for the undue delays in introducing rationing and all other non-monetary direct controls needed to mobilize fully all available productive resources. Lloyd George's attack on him after the First World War because of his failure to gauge Britain's physical strength to wage war seems only too justified.

and the Treasury implicitly condemned its own attempts at maintaining a sort of sham freedom in foreign payments, I wrote: 'The Government—and in this complicated field as in so many others, this exclusively means the Civil Service—were unable to free themselves of their peacetime prejudices and analyse afresh the problems which were thrust on them by the war and which they could not escape. They denied that the problems existed. They resisted all change. They countered criticism by statements as complacent as they were misleading. Finally, when they were driven in a sector to accept the critics' policy, in their fundamental resistance to that very policy they robbed it of most of its merits by a continued lack of imagination, initiative and capacity for planning ahead'. Is this not also a faithful picture of British post-war policy at home and overseas?

How many of our five or six unnecessary dollar crises were caused by complacency similar to that which led to the return to gold and to the underestimate of Hitler's menace is not yet clear. But the impression that the pattern of the inter-war years is repeating itself is all but overwhelming. The lesson which emerges for instance, with irresistible force from the proceedings of the Tribunal appointed to inquire into the so-called Bank Leak is the casualness, if not frivolity and complete absence of expert knowledge or awareness in the highest reaches of the policy-making machine on the occasion of the 1957 crisis. In the con-versations and exchanges which have emerged from their usual well-preserved darkness of discretion, it would be difficult to find a relevant and intellectually coherent observation. The question of why gold losses mounted when the current balance of payments was showing a steady improvement was, as far as the correspon-dence was published, not even once touched upon. In proposing the remedial measures it was not questioned why a fall in income and outlay and especially domestic investment should be used as a main weapon when the problem of gold losses arose mainly out of a speculative attack on sterling combined with large British exports of capital. Yet an increase in capital investment and thus of productive capacity and productivity was the only safe way of assuring a balance of international payments at the same time as increasing standards of life to which the Government was pledged.

And while the veil of discretion has not yet been lifted of the detailed history of the earlier misadventures,[1] we know already that the 1951 disaster of Labour could have been prevented had not the statistical material on which the Labour Government relied been fatally misleading. In 1952–3, the country's bankruptcy as a result of the operation 'Robot' (return to complete convertibility) was only avoided because Mr. Churchill—unlike Dr. Dalton or Mr. Attlee—refused to trust the dilettantes at the Treasury and listened to the courageous warnings of Sir Donald MacDougall, who was brought in from Oxford to advise him. And there was, even before the last crisis, the discomfiture of 1954–5, this time of a Tory Cabinet, mainly as a result of the Treasury-launched doctrine of a 'floating pound', which led to an attack on sterling and the eclipse of Mr. Butler, and at last induced Mr. Macmillan to protest feebly that he was supposed to catch trains by last year's Bradshaw. In the end he too succumbed and continued the policy of stifling investment and thus undermining British strength and economic prospects.

[1] It is difficult for an outsider to gauge the quality and impact of advice to Ministers from the 'official level'. Only when some incident results in the appointment of a Select Committee or Tribunal when—once in a generation— a Royal Commission or Committee (such as the Macmillan Committee, on which Keynes served) investigates a special aspect of policy, can he throw a hurried glance or two behind the scenes, so well-guarded in this country by discretion and the Criminal Code. Even then the coherence of the Establishment tactfully conceals much important detail. More could be learned of the reality of the working of the city and the policy-making organs through the so-called 'Leak' Tribunal than from all respectable textbooks put together. Apart from such windfalls the most revealing documentation can be gleaned from the published musing of retired Civil Servants. Sir F. Leith-Ross's meditations on convertibility are as indicative in this respect as Mr. Kelf-Cohen's rather surprising statistical mistakes in the field of nationalized coal, on which he seems to have advised ministers (*Nationalization in Britain. The end of a dogma.* London 1958, esp. pp. 41, 43 and 46) and assertions which are based—with complete self-confidence—on superficial errors of analysis (esp. pp. 52 and pp. 65–6). Each in its way represents overwhelmingly strong links in the argument in favour of changing the present machinery of policy-making. A surprising exception to the rule of silence on the part of serving Civil Servants (apart from their defence of Government policy on television) is represented by Sir Edgar Cohen's recent defence of the so-called Free Trade Area proposals (*Board of Trade Journal No. 7* 1958, pp. 975–78). Sir Edgar showed complete unawareness of the flagrant contradictions of his case and unawareness of the resistance he was facing (e.g. the illegitimate contrast between the effect of protection of industry and agriculture (p. 977) or the impact effect on British industry of German, or on that of the less developed countries of British, competition). He was even less clear of the implications of failure or of the need to have an alternative policy. In this he is a worthy successor of those British experts who torpedoed the Ouchy Convention of 1931 on the plea of non-

Nor is a comparison with other countries more reassuring, all points to the contrary. Do the results of Anglo-American negotiations (when conducted by regular Civil Servants and not dons brought into the Service) sustain the claim that British officials are superior to their American counterparts? Only too often gross blunders on the official level were only averted by ministerial expertise. There is striking contrast between the American debt settlement in 1924 and the return to the Gold Standard, where the ministers concerned were not experts, and the negotiations leading to the setting up of the European Payments Union where Mr. Gaitskell, himself an expert, was able to rescue the British interests at the last moment. Many more recent examples spring to mind.[1] The fact that there has been no post-war Chancellor whose tenure did not end in crisis and discomfiture

[1] The Smouha scandal, the cavalier oversight of British possessions in Egypt is only the most recent. It was said to be due to Egyptian trickery. But as the *Economist* points out on publication of the agreement (March 7 1959, p. 854):

'The other surprise is the extraordinary careless drafting of the English version of the agreement. Although the Foreign Office has had two and a half years to collect information about the British owners of property in Egypt, the list annexed to the agreement looks like mere clumsy transliterations of the details produced by the other side. The result in places is bizarre enough to be worthy of the attention of Mr. Paul Jennings. Some of the unfortunate property owners may yet have trouble from this source in establishing their claims.'

and this quite apart from the refusal of the British Government to pay the difference between the true value of the properties and the low lump sum compensation. The negotiations leading up to the Reparations Agreement after the Second World War showed what trouble can be caused if a classical scholar misunderstands a complicated economic theory: the British attitude was determined not so much by the resistance against Russia but by the fear that German reparation payment out of current production would ruin British industry. We could have done with such ruin since 1945. In the Bonn Agreements, giving Western Germany full sovereignty, the question of the maintenance of British forces was left so much in the air (and not for political reasons because Britain then still had the whip-hand through its veto) that in subsequent years British Ministers had to go cap in hand to the defeated ex-enemy. In the negotiations on the finance of NATO rearmament in Lisbon the British representative 'wise man' accepted a contribution wholly out of line with the relative capacities to bear the burden. The list could be continued almost endlessly.

---

discrimination while preparing for the Ottawa Preferential System. Sir Frank Lee's (The Permanent Secretary) recent utterances on the work of the Board of Trade (Stamp Memorial Lecture 1958) only strengthen the impression of grave weakness on vital points of the policy-making machine.

should make the present and prospective holders of the office pause a little.

Even the most complacent defenders of the *status quo*, however, have begun to appreciate the need for a change. The appointment of the Radcliffe Committee and the reorganization undertaken at the Treasury, separating formally the responsibility for economic policy-making from the management of personnel, by appointing two Joint Secretaries, are indications of the growing realization of this need, though they are pitifully insufficient to cope with the problem before Britain. In the present context I shall confine my attention strictly to the problem for the democratic control of the bureaucracy though this should not be taken to imply that the trend towards increasingly irresponsible and largely uncontrolled oligarchy of our Party system does not pose equally menacing questions in our national life.[1]

V. *The Mandarin's Paradise*

The reasons for all these failures of our bureaucracy, for the unnecessary weakness of Britain, are not difficult to find. They derive ironically perhaps *from the very success of the boldness of the effort of the Victorian reformer* to give Britain an administrative personnel for a Nightwatchman State presiding over the breathtaking expansion of private industrial capitalism. While its very virtues prevent thorough reform, the change in the essence of economic life has made it unfit to deal with any of the new problems.

We have seen that the fundamental changes we have had in the organization of our higher bureaucracy in this century make it less capable in a modern world. There is a growing centralization enforced by the power of patronage of the Permanent Secretary of the Treasury (now one of the Joint Secretaries) in his capacity as the Head of the Civil Service, the formal acceptance of the supremacy of Administrators who have no professional training, their rapid mobility between departments, and a change in

---

[1] I should like to call attention to Mr. R. Crossman's brilliant essay *Socialism and the New Despotism* which sweeps the whole position (Fabian Tract No. 298).

recruitment favouring the smooth,[1] extrovert conformist with good connexions and no knowledge of modern problems, or of up-to-date techniques of getting that information.

In theory, no doubt, horizontal mobility, the availability of the best talent for the most important tasks, is desirable. But Professor Robson's dutiful exclamation 'We do not want to consign a Civil Servant to a specialized type of job, say finance or establishment work, for life—heaven forbid!' is surely a trifle over-dramatic and misses the point completely. After all, most of the people outside the Civil Service are consigned for life to do much the same job and grin and bear it. Only exceptional people can take on new jobs at a late stage of their career and make a success of them. No one would be mad enough to advocate the periodic interchange of dentists and surgeons, solicitors and barristers, engineers and musicians.[2]

Yet surely the problems which most of these professions encounter are simple in comparison with the complexities of the social and economic system in a modern state, above all of a Welfare State, with which administration has to deal in a more and more positive manner. Moreover, these problems, far from becoming more universal, are increasingly demanding specialized knowledge. Yet, far from acquiring such specialized knowledge, far from making ample use of available experts in the Civil Service itself, in the Universities and the City, the dominant branch of the Civil Service has become more and more generalized and, what is worse, more exclusive.

The time is long past when snap answers could be conjured up out of pure intelligence. The Minister must be provided with ample information based on a knowledge not merely of the problems in their historical setting but also the personal equations involved. If the university training of the higher Civil Servant was not technically relevant to their jobs, there is a pressing need, and not merely in the technical-economic

---

[1] Attempts have been made, by the indefatigable penmen of the bureaucracy, to defend the drift towards conformity and the measures causing it as an inevitable requirement of living in a new and dangerous age. So far as Britain is concerned there can be no doubt that the consequential deadening effect which eliminates originality has resulted in a relative decline in Britain's strength and influence.

[2] This rapid change in assignments is especially damaging in the Foreign Service and Colonial Office, and in the Central Economic Departments.

departments, for thorough specialized training at the beginning of their career, followed by arrangements for refresher courses like a Staff College, and a fairly specialized career in the service. What we get in fact is a two-tier dilettantism. It may well happen that both the Permanent Secretary and the Minister arrive simultaneously at a new department. Neither of them has made an intensive study of the problems with which they have to deal, or know the personalities and the social background. How purposive positive policy can be formed under these conditions is a mystery, or rather it would be a mystery if purposive policy were formed. At best, the departments drift in the maelstrom of events, trying to keep afloat or barely so.

The unsuitability of the present organization of the British Administration at the higher policy-making level is the principal explanation of the drift towards *laissez-faire*.[1] In a planned economy, the crossword-puzzle mind, reared on mathematics at Cambridge or Greats at Oxford, has only a limited outlet. They must defend themselves against a system in which positive action is in order because they can only express themselves by transferring decisions from the realm of economic realities into the sphere of pseudo-moral philosophy. This is only possible in a 'free' economy where the State has no, or at most very limited, functions. Complicated problems are then cheerfully solved by the application of so-called 'general principles'. Instead of detached thinking, we get metaphysical sermons on 'the need for a collective approach' or 'willing the means to NATO' (i.e., adopting American policy uncritically). The end products of these dialectics are the drive towards convertibility, the dissolution of the Sterling Area, dear money and the slowing down of productive investment—the roots, in short, of all our present discontents. The fact that the Treasury controls senior appointments, and that Ministers are busy men, does the rest. Mr. Harold Wilson aptly put it: 'Whoever

---

[1] Though the desire, put into apt phrases by the inimitable felicity of Mr. Butler (as reported by *The Times*, 15 March 1958) to prevent a future Labour Government from being able to protect the national interests by re-instituting some of the controls abandoned, must also have played an important role. The new 'freedom' to keep Trade Unions 'in their place' and to oppose Labour by an extra-constitutional veto of a currency crisis was purchased by having to impose dear money and suffer some diminution of profits—along with unemployment. The inevitable threat to the relative international power and influence of Britain of this system does not seem to have been realized or, if realized, given much weight.

is in Office, the Whigs are in power.' By now, as Robert Boothby always knew, and Mr. Butler, Mr. Macmillan and last, but not least, Mr. Thorneycroft must by now suspect, even the fate of a Tory Minister is not quite safe in the hands of their present advisers.[1]

VI. Labour and Establishment

If Tories, who have the confidence and co-operation of the City and the great industrial oligarchs, twice have almost come a cropper in the impact of Whiggish policies, Labour of course was, and remains, far more menaced by them and in more ways than one. Not only must its leaders guard against the extra-constitutional veto of a financial confidence crisis, but in order to stand up against the constant hostile propaganda of the press and the advertisers, they must show considerable material successes only attainable by purposive action. Otherwise they will be worn down and overthrown.

The problem is by no means new. It has haunted the Liberal Party and especially its Radical members in the last century. It returned with a vengeance when the first Labour Leader became a Cabinet Minister. Writing of John Burns, Mr. (later Sir R. C. K.) Ensor gave a plastic account of what was to be repeated in 1924, and again in 1929–31[2].

'What happens when a minister lacking those qualities (of determination of overcoming the discouragements of high officials) holds a key position was abundantly illustrated after 1903, by the case of John Burns and the local government board.

---

[1] For a revealing story of the misleading advice given to Tory Ministers, especially Mr. Butler, cf. Mr. Shonfield's booklet *British Economic Policy Since the War* (Penguin 1958, esp. 169–172; 180–4; 188–227).

Open opposition of the Civil Service to party policy might be preferred to political bias disguised as objective expert opinion. There is no reason to doubt the sincerity with which these beliefs are held, both in Economic Departments and the Bank. Indeed, one might talk of righteousness rather than mere sincerity.

[2] The failure of the 1929–31 Labour Government with its feeble Economic Advisory Council on which its bitter enemies were in a large majority (just as on all Committees then and afterwards appointed by Labour Ministers), is the most deplorable of these experiences.

No other department bestrode more fields where progress was needed—poor law, municipal government, housing, town planning, public health. Unfortunately, as we saw above, it had been so constituted in 1871 that its dominant tradition became that of the old poor law board—a tradition of cramping the local authorities and preventing things from being done. When Burns went there, the officials at its head included some able men deeply imbued with this spirit; and the ex-demagogue, sincere and upright, but without administrative experience and lacking either the education or the kind of ability that might have saved him, fell at once under their control. The result was that for nine years, during which the home office, the board of trade, and the board of education were all helping the nation to go forward, the local government board, though it had the greatest opportunities of all, remained for the most part anti-progressive.'[1]

The timidity and conventional conformity of most past Labour leaders did not exhaust itself in their relation to the bureaucracy.[2] But it is this aspect that perhaps illustrates their failure at its most glaring. Mr. (now Sir) Roy Harrod inimitably describes the process.

'Professor Beer reckons 1947 a critical date, when Sir Stafford Cripps, having been for a brief period Minister for Economic Affairs, also became Chancellor, taking his responsibility for economic planning and his set-up with him. It could be argued that in the saving of the country from a jarring discordant form of Socialism, harsh bureaucracy ... the bringing of economic planning—under the aegis, I don't know whether it would be fair to say under the nose, of Sir Stafford Cripps —into the sphere of the sage and mellow influence of Treasury traditions was a much more decisive step than the Conservative victory in 1951.'

The sage and mellow influence of Treasury influence has resulted in five or six severe crises, reduced the rate of economic

---

[1] R. C. K. Ensor, *England 1870–1917*, p. 516–7.

[2] It is fascinating to recall that it was Mr. Attlee who appointed the most reactionary Lord Chief Justice and the most obscurantist Archbishop in modern British history, the last after Churchill had named Temple, the greatest of the English Christian Socialists.

growth below that of any major European country and continues to stifle capital investment. But there is no doubt that planning was avoided.

The two post-war Labour Chancellors who had ample political power (Mr. Gaitskell already inherited an impossible position), Dr. Dalton and Sir Stafford Cripps stand out—as it is now clear[1]— in their complete inability to grasp the importance of the problem despite much public grandiloquence for the benefit of their followers. The need was obvious for a thorough reform of the general policy-making machine at the Treasury[2] and the Bank of England, even before the Parker Tribunal uncovered their jejune amateurishness.[3] The evidence of the inter-war and war time failures of the Treasury and the Bank was overwhelming. Dr. Dalton in introducing the Bill nationalizing the Bank was as explicit and characteristically robust in his claims as he was magnificent in his promise:

'By this Bill we ensure a smooth and efficient working of our financial and banking system in order to meet the new needs of the future. This Government has a mandate for a five year plan of economic development . . . *to lay the foundations of an economic plan for this country and a new social order.* . . .'

(My italics)

[1] It is, perhaps comprehensively, not quite clear to Dr. Dalton, who does not seem to have benefited much from the experiences of the past twelve years. In the *Fabian Journal* of March 1958, he writes, contrasting the present situation with 1925, when Lord Norman raised the Bank Rate against the protest of the then Chancellor, Mr. Churchill: 'All this is changed now, as a result of my Bank of England Act of 1946. Today the Chancellor in disagreements with the Bank, always has the last word. Under Section 4 of that "streamlined socialist statute" as I venture to describe it, the Chancellor may issue directions to the Bank of England, or through the Bank of England, to any Bank in Britain. In practice, probably no direction will ever need to be issued. It will only be necessary to hint at the existence of this power.' In point of fact it is rather doubtful how far the 'streamlined' powers which are ill-defined and unbacked by penalties can in fact be enforced in a crisis.

[2] In contrast to the Economic Section.

[3] Lord Norman realized that for an effective carrying out of his policy of preserving a 'politically independent' (in plain English ultra Liberal-Conservative) Central Bank he had to reorganize the Bank of England ruthlessly. And he showed no mercy to tradition in attaining objectives. But his objective was not 'to lay the foundations of an *economic* plan for this country or a new social order'. It was to control economic policy through the monetary system.

Mr. Bevin in a powerful speech commending the Trade Disputes and Trade Unions Bill[1] did not mince his words as to whom he regarded as the authors of the General Strike and inter-war unemployment. He put them squarely on the directors of the Bank of England and more especially Sir Otto Niemeyer.

And what happened? Dr. Dalton instructed the Governor-to-be and the Parliamentary Counsel to "reassure" Parliament that there would be no change in the control of the Bank and when the Act had been passed reappointed all those permanent directors who were prominently associated with Mr. Norman, in particular Sir Otto Niemeyer.[2] In the sequel the Bank's influence grew and Dr. Dalton committed himself to a hopeless attempt at the complete convertibility of sterling. In the ensuing crisis Britain—as at the beginning of the war and many times since—lost hundreds of millions of gold bitterly needed for reconstruction, and was only saved from grave unemployment by the Marshall Plan. The crisis had been foreseen by almost everybody, including the American officials responsible who counselled caution.

When, as a result of Dr. Dalton's budget slip, Sir Stafford succeeded him as Chancellor, he continued his policy of excluding progressive economists from the Board (despite the precedent set by Lord Keynes' appointment during the war-time Coalition Government), elevated Mr. Cobbold (who was Norman's special protegé) to the Governorship, and was not less misleading about the real position than his predecessor.

At the House he proudly declared that the Bank was his 'creature'. The next day he apologetically described this claim as

[1] *Hansard* Vol. 419. Col. 701.

[2] Minutes of proceedings of the Select Committee on the Bank of England Bill, Nov. 20 1945, H.o.C. 24, p. 11, Answer 116.

Witness (Lord Catto): The Court of Directors of the Bank will carry on the affairs of the Bank much as it has done in the past, and I do not think, and it has not occurred to me, that there would be any interference with anything of that kind.

Sir Cyril Radcliffe: May I say, on behalf of the Government, that that is as we understand the position too. The Corporation, with all its management and finance, goes on as before.

Captain Crookshank: If it is not abundantly clear it might be made the subject of an amendment, perhaps.

Witness (Lord Catto): I think it is quite clear, Captain Crookshank, that there is no question about that.

a 'jest'.[1] If it was a joke it certainly was a costly one for Labour and the nation.

The impact of the 'Establishment' was, if anything, even more pernicious on Labour's Colonial policy.[2] The well-meaning intentions of Mr. Creech-Jones were frustrated on almost all levels. Politically the conflict with the countries under our protection was continuous. In Palestine, Cyprus, and the Gold Coast the old pattern of colonial discontent and violence repeated itself. The Labour Government was almost entrapped into accepting the Central African Federation. The value of a closer connexion with Britain was not made manifest by skilful planning of economic development, provision of markets and technical help and facilities for education.[3]

Where attempts were made at planning development, lack of expert knowledge or downright hostility to Labour's conception of policy frustrated success. The dependent areas became the happy hunting ground of extreme *laisser-faire* economists and displaced imperial administrators. The inability of the Colonial Office to obtain essential supplies and capital for the dependent areas retarded development. Indeed a number of these areas exported capital to Britain though the bulk-purchase agreements negotiated immediately after the war were (unlike the wartime guarantees) concluded at terms far too favourable to Britain. When world prices fell and there would have been the greatest need for security of markets Britain discontinued bulk purchases altogether. The halting method of liberation resulted in many economically far too small areas becoming independent instead of joining larger units. From Arabia to West Africa, South East Asia to East Africa

[1] Minutes of Evidence of the Tribunal, Exhibit 10, p. 208, 2nd col. Mr. Cobbold's Memorandum: "The Bank of England is not as is sometimes suggested, a mere operating department under the Treasury. This suggestion has been fed over recent years by quotation of a reference by a very great Chancellor of the Exchequer to the Bank as 'his creature', a phrase which the Chancellor told me on the following day he had used lightly and in jest."

[2] In sharp contrast to policy towards India, Ceylon and Burma. Mr. Attlee had familiarized himself with the problems of these countries in his younger days and carried out a policy which he had then conceived. But as a socialist one wonders whether negative 'liberation' was enough. There is no doubt whatever that at that late stage no other policy was possible. Indian allegiance to a closer connexion with Britain had long been lost.

[3] I have dealt with this problem at greater length in one of the *Fabian Colonial Essays* (London 1959).

this process of Balkanization threatens the future of vast and poverty-stricken areas. The Establishment succeeded in exporting the disdain of technical and mass-education so bitterly needed in territories struggling to emerge from primeval poverty and indoctrinating them in the social (rather than intellectual) snobbery and 'apartheid' of Oxbridge, in societies where tremendous pressure would in any case be necessary to overcome such centrifugal tendencies. The sprouting new colleges all over the Commonwealth seem stumbling blocks rather than aids to general development.

The lesson of 1945–51 seems unmistakeable. *Mr. Attlee had immense advantages.* He had a Parliamentary majority unparalleled since 1906, and a clear mandate for far-reaching reforms. *He had, what was not ever enjoyed by any Socialist Government anywhere, a fully working war economic system of direct controls at his disposal, built up in the teeth of the vested interests and the bureaucracy.* In five years he went far in divesting himself of this power. The repeated failures in economic planning, despite grandiloquent promises, did the rest. Though his reforms, within the rather narrow limits set, were admirable, he wasted his majority by 1951, without achieving a new social order or even economic stability. Had he not possessed the war-time system of controls his Government might have met its fate quicker.[1]

If a clue is to be found for the fundamental failure of the 1945 experiment it might well be found in Earl Attlee's revealing exchange of letters with Mr. Jo Grimond (*The Times*, 26 September 1958). Mr. Grimond, in a speech to the Liberal Party Conference, referred to "the patronage and privilege by which both Socialists and Tories manipulate our politics" and said "Far too many prizes in the law, the Church, commerce, and social life go to those whom the ruling clique find agreeable."

Earl Attlee (who, with his inimitable astringency, recently disposed of the late Prof. Laski's insight into politics by saying "he never quite got the hang of it") could have patiently explained to Mr. Grimond that no political leader, indeed, no political party in Britain or indeed anywhere else could do without patronage.[2] He could have told him that policy—let alone a policy

---

[1] The problem of 1951, was after all, not so far removed from 1931.

[2] Earl Attlee's (K.G., O.M., C.H.) disdain of lesser men's yearning for distinctions was expressed sharply in his contribution to the *Political Quarterly*

of reform—can hardly be successfully carried on for any length
of time without having an Establishment at the command of the
Party. Indeed, he could have reminded him that Liberals knew
this full well even before Mr. Lloyd George strengthened his war-
chest by granting honours to helpers. Certain key positions of
power need for success to be held by sympathizers. The Suez
failure shows what happens if a Government scorns even a basically favourable Establishment. Nor did Earl Attlee say that a
Labour Leader who—like himself—had struggled towards
Socialism by way of Christianity, is entitled to ask whether the
social beliefs held by the person promoted were compatible with
his own ethical views. If one has moral convictions should one
elevate what is at best questionable, at worst wicked? He did
neither. He wrote:

'I was for six years responsible for recommendations to the
episcopal bench. I have no knowledge of the political opinions
of any one of the bishops appointed during my period of office.
I was responsible for a large number of appointments to the
judiciary and of promotions. Of these the only ones whose
political views I know were Lord Somervell and Lord Reid,
Conservatives, and Lord Birkett, a Liberal.'

He could have added to this list most of the boards of nationalized industries (including the Bank of England) and some of his
so-called Planning Board. Under the circumstances it must be
reckoned to the credit of the—relative—tolerance of British
society (and the system of controls evolved during the war) that
the Labour régime was as successful, and lasted as long as it did.

(1959). Lord Attlee's attitude seems a revolutionary innovation. The British
two party system has in the past been broadly based in the existence of two
alternative Establishments. If one of the parties forgoes creating its own Establishment and promotes its rivals' adherents without due regard to their social
attitudes, it is liable to forfeit its chances of remaining a vigorous body, able
to draw its personnel from all classes.

VII. *The Outline of a Solution*

If the analysis of the causes of our weakness and failure due to inadequate policy-making is not very difficult, the history of the last half century seems clearly to point to the solution of our discontents. There were three occasions on which the British Government either initiated or was forced to initiate positive policies from scratch. The first was the great reform era of the Liberal Cabinet after 1906; the second and third occurred during the two World Wars. The Labour Government of 1945 was not confronted with this problem: it could build on an existing system of war economies.[1]

Two lessons stand out. The first is that Ministers who tried to accomplish their aims while maintaining 'business as usual' utterly failed and soon disappeared. The example so plastically pictured by Ensor of Burns was repeated again and again, especially in war-time. Asquith and his Liberal colleagues, in particular MacKenna and Runciman, failed in ultimate analysis because they did not perceive this. Chamberlain and his Tory friends, culpable as they were, were, as we already said, equally badly served.

The second lesson is equally clear. Ensor describes the process of reform:

'Though the bills dealing with sweating decasualization and unemployment no more emanated from a cabinet minister's brain than had the 1902 Education Act, signal credit is due, as in that case to Balfour, so in these to Churchill and Lloyd George, for having, as ministers, brought them to the statute book. As a rule only a minister of high intelligence, capable of discounting the discouragements of high officials and fellow ministers, will put through measures of this kind.'[2]

It was *outsiders*, recruited for this purpose, such as William (now Lord) Beveridge who put through the innovations. And as it was in 1906–12 so it remained in the Wars. *Whenever any effort*

[1] It did, however, dismantle the war-time controls erected against the will of the bureaucracy.

[2] R. C. K. Ensor, *England 1870–1914*, p. 516.

had to be organized, indeed palpably threatening disaster averted,
outsiders had to be recruited to take charge.[1]

In the First World War the Ministry of Munitions, Shipping
and Food was manned by them. As the Second World War
approached the bureaucracy vowed not to permit the repetition
of such interference. In preparing the blueprints for war-time
adminstration, under Sir Horace Wilson (woefully inadequate as
they turned out to be after the real war started), outsiders were
carefully relegated to subordinate positions. *By the end of the war*
there was no department concerned with the war which was not in fact,
if not even formally, headed by people recruited from outside. And in
the Board of Trade rationing and industrial planning, the tasks
which needed positive action were put through by such distinguished outside recruits as Hugh Gaitskell, Douglas Jay and
Richard Kahn. In conditions where the nation's will to live
awakens and demands positive action the mandarins must be
displaced. They are a hindrance to survival in policy making,
though, when properly supervised, they often are superb in its
execution.

Both Lloyd George and Churchill came to realize it.[2] They
both used outside advice in the First World War and Churchill
continued the tradition in the Second and also after 1951.

1. We have seen that the basic weakness of the present structure
of the Civil Service, which to a large extent explains the weakness
of personnel, is its structure, favouring centralization and thus
dilettantism. No one in his senses would run an organization of
some 4,500 higher and potentially policy-making people, charged
with positive and complicated duties, on the exact pattern which
was shaped for a compact small service of a couple of hundred
men, dedicated to the task of preserving a negative state.

The complete irresponsibility which is derived from the

---

[1] In view of the present difficulties caused by the Bank of England, it is
interesting to recall Lloyd George's condemnation of its inanity in the fateful
summer days of 1914 and his backing of Bonar Law who had to threaten the
then Governor of the Bank with dismissal before he altered its policy which
disregarded national interests.

[2] It is interesting that it was Lloyd George who had all this experience in
the Board of Trade, Treasury and Ministry of Munitions as well as Downing
Street, who sanctioned the fatal strengthening of the Treasury. In his later life
he bitterly regretted this decision and blamed, as I mentioned before, his depen-
dence on the Conservatives and the bureaucrats, whose hatred of his Kindergarten knew no bounds.

Establishment of a closed estate dependent *de facto* only on its own chiefs, and in particular on the Head of the Service, must be ended by the well tried methods of earlier (and wiser) political leaders. It is inadmissible that the British bureaucracy should remain the only large scale organization that is run on the basis of complete *de facto* concentration of power.[1] The power of the Headships of the Treasury and Civil Service has grown to menace the future of the country. He can, as Sir Edward (now Lord) Bridges has demonstrated, determine the tone of the whole of the Establishment. He can, if mistaken, through constant influence in promotion in the Civil Service and the nationalized industries and national shareholdings, create a threat to national survival. No single man ought to possess that power.

Now in theory, there is a Committee and its sub-Committees which are supposed to perform the balanced control of the bureaucracy, and at the same time ensure its subservience to the democratic will: the Cabinet. But we have seen that in general Ministerial supervision breaks down through the monolithic scepticism of the Bureaucracy and its capacity to overwhelm with papers and arguments the overworked and isolated politicians. *Without tackling this basic problem no makeshift arrangement through the recruitment of experts can possibly work.* Nor can it be tackled if the Ministers' will to survive and succeed does not assert itself. They must acknowledge that they (at best helped by a couple of junior Ministers) cannot subdue and control huge departments fiercely asserting their rights.

The first task is therefore to put the job of the Head of the Civil Service into Commission and see to it that no over-mighty subject should usurp as much power. *Advice to the Prime Minister and to the Cabinet on higher appointments in the service should be tendered by a Committee of Senior Civil Servants.* In the main shifts between Departments should be exceptional, and subject to detailed explanation to the Cabinet.

2. When this has been done similar reforms should be put through all major Departments: they should be put under a *Committee of equal Permanent Officials* who are to advise the Minister as a body on all major questions. Each of these Civil

---

[1] The American in theory is even more concentrated. In practice the number of political and temporary appointments is sufficient to re-establish its corporate character,

Servants, as in America, should be in charge of a part of the office (or certain functions entrusted to it if they can be separated). In this way there is hope that the advice tendered will be informed and not merely inspired. The power-position between Ministers and Civil Servants will begin to approach the picture painted in constitutional fiction.

3. The policy that *posts in nationalized or nationally owned industries* are increasingly used to compensate retiring or displaced Civil Servants must also be ended. The American system which demands Senate approval of important posts has led to—though it has also prevented—much mischief. While its slavish imitation would be uncalled for, there is (also for other reasons) a good case for having special House of Commons Committees established to supervise these industries and firms. These could be informed of appointments and given opportunities to ask questions. Much abuse would automatically cease if queries would threaten.

4. A number of consequential further reforms will be necessary. It seems, first of all, essential to create a *Ministry of the Budget* to exercise continuous and expert financial control instead of the present fitful amateurish annual reviews of expenditure which only work on niggling points[1] (like preventing the appointment of a Governor when someone else is still nominally the holder of the office). Economic policy can then be decided on its own merits and financial control exercised in a systematic way informed by expert knowledge of the technical detail.

5. It will be equally necessary, in the second place, to strengthen *expert knowledge in the policy-making machine*. In the following I must restrict myself to the problem of *economic* policy-making of which I have first hand knowledge. But what I say is equally applicable (though perhaps has less general implication) in the social and political (including especially foreign political) field.

The problem of economic policy-making falls into a short and long term question.

a. To solve our *long run problem* steps must be taken to end the discouragement of expert—especially economic—knowledge, which is now implicit in the method of recruitment as it is now being worked. It gets around quite quickly that classical scholars are preferred by the Treasury and that,

[1] A most interesting (but unfortunately rather narrow-minded) criticism has been made by a recent (1958) report of the Select Committee on Expenditure.

even if an economist slips in, he is promptly put on some soul-destroying task to 'break his conceit'. It would seem essential to restore the importance of purely competitive examination. A certain number of places could (as in most Oxford Colleges) be reserved for 'Commoners' who might make 'good College men'. But this number should certainly not exceed twenty-five per cent and should preferably be restricted to less. Economics training, moreover, should be made more attractive as a way into the Service through a modification of the Civil Service Examination system and some organic system should be introduced, as in France, for a compulsory one-year course in economics, sociology, etc., for all civil servants in departments dealing with economic matters, to be followed by an examination before final establishment.

b. In the *short run* several ways are open to remedy the desperate shortage of economic and statistical know-how. The Economic Section of the Treasury must be enlarged and its members incorporated into the established regular administrative class. The section should be made directly responsible to the Chancellor. It is intolerable that such scarce (and exceedingly valuable) intellectual resources as exist, should be short-circuited as they have been in the recent past. In addition, young economists should be recruited into economic departments, who have had some academic training and research, and should be able to make their way into the highest reaches of the Civil Service at least as easily as anyone else. The present system by which highly trained young men are put to deal with footling routine matters is a waste of scarce resources which the country certainly cannot afford.

But it would be foolish to expect that economic expertise itself will solve the problem of economic policy-making. Professor (now Lord) Robbins'—or Mr. George Schwartz's, or their pupils'—advice would not be better, and might be worse than that of those dilettantes who try to play by the ear and who might, by mistake, learn better tunes.[1] It should

[1] Though both under Sir Stafford Cripps and since, much of the policy-making mischief was influenced by *The Economist* and the pundits of the London School of Economics.

have become obvious—though it is strenuously denied by the 'Establishment' (not excluding Lord Attlee)—that economic policy-making is *not* a scientific exercise which admits objective impartiality. It is an art inseparable from political assumptions.

Thus it is essential that expert opinion from the outside, sharing the point of view of the Government of the day should be employed also at senior levels. Only they could enforce adequate consideration and positive elaboration of policies from the *point of view of the government of the day*. The American system which replaces the Heads of Divisions with politically trusted experts whenever the Party in power changes has worked much better than the British. It should, however, be made less abrupt. There is good reason why the Permanent staff of a Ministry should remain permanent and political favouritism should not poison personal relationships within ministries.

A compromise is in order.

Ministers in charge of large Departments must at least be armed with private offices and experts recruited from outside and dependent on the minister. The example of the most successful leaders of Britain in peace and in war, Lloyd George and Churchill, in their days of success and confidence, shows what can be done by this relatively minor reform.

In addition—and here again the example of the U.S. gives confidence to the recommendation—a small and expert Council of Economic Advisors or Investment Board responsible to the Chancellor or Cabinet should be established, charged with the elaboration of longer term policies. Whether or not Britain will emerge from the present quasi-stagnation will mainly depend on whether she will be successful in transforming herself into a dynamic high investment economy.[1]

---

[1] This was recognized by the Labour Government. In the memorandum accompanying the Investment Control and Guarantees Bill, introduced by Dr. Dalton in January 1946, it was stated: 'It is the policy of His Majesty's Government to establish and maintain a proper balance between the economic resources of the community and the demands upon them. This means that priority must always be assured for those projects of capital development which are of the greatest importance in the national interest. It will, therefore, be

THE APOTHEOSIS OF THE DILETTANTE

6. Once the Central Administration is reformed steps could be taken to bring the Bank of England under closer control of the Treasury and infuse into the Court intellectual influences and economic knowledge which might counterbalance the City point of view which now dominates it. Central banking is not concerned with granting sound loans but with the economic destiny of the country. It would be a grave mistake for a Labour Cabinet to rely on the hope of being able to appoint a Governor who, at one stroke, would be able to transform the Bank into a supporter of a Labour Government. It would be a graver mistake to think that the appointment of a Court of exclusive full-time membership would solve the problem. The appointment of a quasi-independent, permanent full-time Court would make the Bank more and not less independent of the Treasury, and subject the 'full-time' directors more and not less to the Governor. Institutions have their own traditions and laws of development.

---

essential to plan both private and public investment, not merely in the narrow financial sense of controlling borrowing, but also in the wider sense of planning real capital development of all kinds.

Within the limits of such guidance, however, there should be the fullest co-operation between the Government, the public and private undertakings responsible for capital development, and the agencies providing the finance. His Majesty's Government are anxious to make this co-operation more close and effective than hitherto.

With this end in view His Majesty's Government have decided to set up a National Investment Council. The Chairman will be the Chancellor of the Exchequer. The members of the Council will include the Governor of the Bank of England, the Chairman of the London Stock Exchange, the Chairmen of the Capital Issues Committee and the Public Works Loan Board, and a number of other persons chosen for their wide knowledge and experience of financial, economic and industrial questions. . . ."

The relaxation of direct control prevented a serious effort at planning investment. Unless draconic steps are taken, including control over the accumulating liquid reserves of private firms—which constitutes the largest part of total finance of industrial investment—and short term finance, little hold can be gained over the monetary side. Only a very small proportion of the total investment, especially total productive investment, is obtained through finance by the capital market, and in most cases financial replacement merely liquidates finance which has been earlier obtained from different sources. The Investment Advisory Board, if it had been a small body of economic and technical experts, could have played an important part in conjunction with Economic Sections of the Cabinet Office, in imparting professional advice to the Chancellor, so entirely lacking at the Treasury. Its constitution was unwieldy and it fell between being a compact body advising the Chancellor and a representative body doing his public relations job for him in a most important field. It had no influence and expired.

The intransigence, as early as Mr. Truman's day, of the U.S. Federal Reserve Board, which has full-time members and depends on a permanent civil service staff, has made orderly economic policy-making even more difficult in the U.S. than it is here. That lesson must be learnt. What is needed is far more intricate than the mere abolition of part-time directors, far more difficult than the *leger-de-main* now contemplated by some people in the Labour party.

The present leadership of the Labour party is more experienced and much more expert than their predecessors. They have lived through 1931 and 1951. They have lived through two wars—and even Crichel Downs. They can have few illusions, and this fact is perhaps the best ground for hope for progressive reform to regain Britain's strength and international influence.

Civil Service reform alone will not restore parliamentary democracy or Cabinet responsibility in Britain. It cannot, by itself create the basis for a successful Socialist Government. It is, however, one of the most essential and fundamental pre-conditions of both. So long as Labour hankers after being accepted by the old 'Establishment', instead of creating its own, so long will it be in an awkward position, forced mainly on the defensive; so long, moreover, will the country remain uneasily poised on the brink of crisis, sinking behind its more dynamic competitors. The Russian system with its vast output of technicians and ever increasing production will overwhelm us as manufacturing exporters, if a break with past traditional errors cannot be made.

It is a challenge to Labour to achieve this and it dare not fail.

The Confidence Trick:

SIR NORMAN TULLIS AND PARTNERS

by *Victor Sandelson*

Age 30. Stockbroker. Author of *The Undergraduate's Guide to the Stock Exchange*. Ex-editor *Granta*. Formerly on the *Financial Times*. Married, one son.

A CRUDELY villainous take-over bid to buy control of Henry Armstrong and Sons, an old-fashioned textile firm, in order to sell its undervalued stock for a large profit, is the subject of a recent melodrama about the workings of finance, *Any Other Business*. It is discovered that on the board of the threatened company is an informer—a 'bloody traitor', as one working (and working-class) director calls him—who has been advising the bidder of the board's plans to defeat him. Suspicion falls on Sir Norman Tullis, the chairman. The traitor is subsequently discovered to be a part-time director, significantly an ignorant and weak-minded politician. Sir Norman (despite severe personal stress all the while, caused by his wife's illness), alone succeeds in foiling the bidder, proving again his cool sagacity to his fellow-directors, and earning anew the affection that the workpeople of Henry Armstrong and Sons are shown to have for him: he defeats the bidder by making a counter-offer for the bidder's own concern, a manoeuvre in which he is backed by his powerful friends in the City.

This rough summary, if possibly unfair to an entertaining piece of theatre, is a useful point of departure for any discussion of the City establishment. Sir Norman is a man of integrity, wealth, influence, education and judgement; his fellow directors, all ordinary fellows, in comparison, may hope to rival him in integrity, but in all his other attributes they are miles apart. And here we have, to start with, a guide to the qualities of a member of the City establishment, and a means to distinguish between him and the Conservative businessman, inside or outside the City.

City men who possess both great wealth and great power are few, often hardly known by the tens of thousands who work in the City, and who are proud of being of the City. It is important to make a distinction between the man who 'does something in the City', whether he be clerk in a merchant's office or, higher up the scale, a prosperous stockbroker, and a City man whose influence is such that he can be said, in a very real way, to help to rule the country. It is not easy to draw a line between them, especially as both share certain attitudes and principles, and are loyal to approximately the same commercial code. Both, for example, affect distaste for 'politics' and 'politicians' in general and Labour Party politicians in particular.

No doubt, a large number of City clerks vote Labour. But 'the City' is notoriously and understandably anti-socialist, and the anti-socialism of the City is probably stronger and more logical than, say, the anti-socialism of the regimental mess. It is the anti-socialism of the City which especially provokes, and is provoked by, the irrational pleasure which Labour back-benchers take in seeing the City embarrassed.

However, although the City is almost uniformly anti-socialist, the instinctive dislike for the City on the part of most Labour Party members is not fundamentally a dislike of the City as a whole; it is a dislike of the enormous financial *power* of the City as vested there in the City establishment, and as representing the heart of the English capitalist structure. This distinction, obvious as it may be, is an important one, especially insofar as it affects the problem of how the City can both function satisfactorily (and to the satisfaction of foreign holders of pounds sterling), and also co-operate with a Labour Government, which is not intending to dismantle the whole capitalist structure of the country. It is worth remembering that the quarrel between the Labour Party and the City is a quarrel between socialists and, as Mr. Fry and Mr. Rudd have written in the *Manchester Guardian*, 'men 10 ft. tall, who are the heads of the big merchant banks and who have the ear of the Governor of the Bank of England before anyone else. . . .'

The fundamental split, to revert to the play, is not between the Labour Party and the directors of Henry Armstrong and Sons; it is between the Labour Party and the influential Sir Norman Tullis. Directors of business concerns all over the country often startle the uninformed observer by the vehemence of their denunciation of 'the City'. Their feelings follow the lines that they and their workpeople toil for years in a sort of unspoken partnership, but that, when for financial reasons, recourse is made to the City, large sums have to be paid out for services which appear to them to be more nominal than real. Their attitude mirrors the fundamental distrust of the businessman for the financier.

Now, a Sir Norman Tullis is not found working in any odd corner of the 'square mile' of the City of London. The printing and newspaper trades in and around Fleet Street are properly part of the City, but few journalists have the ear of the Governor of the Bank of England! Workers, even men of position and substance, in the City merchant firms, the Wool Exchange or the London Metal Exchange, the grain markets or the other commodity markets, are not men 10 ft. tall who can dispute authority with Treasury officials. The City's stockbrokers, although an essential part of the financial district where true power resides, even though perhaps especially suspect to many good Labour Party members, have limited powers for influencing the country's economic policy.

Sir Norman Tullis, a field member of the City establishment, is to be found near, but not in, the Stock Exchange, in one of the head offices of the merchant banks or 'Big Five', at the board of a national insurance company, and on the Court of Directors of the Bank of England itself (see Appendix).

Although there is a great gulf fixed between Sir Norman Tullis and the rest of the City, the City as a whole buttresses his position with wealth and dignity. It provides him with overt support at all times and in turn depends upon him to safeguard its traditions and interests. Sir Norman will undoubtedly have been educated at Eton, and Trinity College, Cambridge. His attitude towards professional politicians will be born of mistrust out of contempt: it may be convenient, for share-policy, to have a Member of Parliament on certain boards, but such men are mere puppets, a safety-valve for the inexplicable emotions of the masses but unimportant as a source of power. His business contacts, inside and outside the City, will be close and numerous, particularly including his many old schoolfellows. In his public life he will be anxious to foster the prosperity of the particular concerns on whose boards he sits, and, more generally, to enhance the commercial and financial power of the City of London—thereby, he tells himself, benefiting the whole country's economy—while maintaining its reputation for efficiency and integrity.

These two words, indeed, are very important to him, as they are to all City men. 'Traditionally', says a reviewer in the *Stock*

Exchange Journal, 'the City of London is a place where there is no need to put a bargain into writing, since it is known that a verbal agreement will certainly be met.' When an inquiry is held into an alleged Bank Rate leak, the Governor of the Bank of England says he hopes that the final result of the tribunal 'may be not only to maintain, but actually to enhance, the reputation of London for financial integrity'. This integrity is second-nature to Sir Norman; he learned it at home, at his public school, and in the City itself.

Since so much of the City's working depends upon the honesty of City men, just as British commercial prestige in the wider world has been built up on trust, it is necessary that in this respect the heart of the City should be irreproachable. And, having mentioned the alleged Bank Rate leak, it is worth adding the words of a Labour Party back bencher in the debate on the Tribunal's findings. 'I do not challenge the integrity and good intentions of the Board of the Bank of England . . . so far as honour is concerned they enjoy the highest reputation for integrity in the world.' These words, significantly, came from one of the few Labour members who has had close contact with the City and really understands its workings.

.   .   .   .   .

It is possible to rise to great heights in the City even if, to start with, one is technically an outsider. The Establishment in Britain has been described as 'a handful of people whose family trees are rooted in the history books'. Yet the late Lord Bracken won astonishing influence in the City though even his obituary notices served only to increase the mystery of his origins. He was, however, exceptional. Sir Norman Tullis sprang from a landed family and would have made himself an equally distinguished career had he chosen the army, the church, or politics, instead of the City. Furthermore, he can have no social ambitions. His family, school and university connections help him to be more useful to his companies, and more efficient as a City man. This is why men of his sort are appointed to the directorships of various boards, in preference to others who have laboriously worked their way through a company to high managerial positions. For companies, whether banking or insurance or industrial, value the social and business connections which a man of the Establishment can bring them.

To praise Sir Norman's integrity is not to claim that there are never times when his loyalties are divided. He, for example, would have been extremely sympathetic towards Mr. W. J. Keswick when the latter at the time of the sterling crisis in the autumn of 1957 wrote sadly to his colleague in Hong Kong, *a propos* of switching from sterling into North American securities: 'Again, this is anti-British and derogatory to sterling but, on balance, if one is free to do so, it makes sense to me'. He would, however, claim that only very rarely does one's commercial loyalty clash with one's patriotism and that, against these isolated incidents, must be weighed the constant strengthening of the British economy by the earnings of the City. The quasi-mystical conviction that the City, in the course of its business, *is necessarily always acting to the benefit of the national economy*, is reinforced by a variety of factors. It is in fact simply the obsolete, long liberal belief that if every citizen would concentrate on improving his own or his company's economic fortunes in legal fashion, he would inevitably be benefiting the national economy. If the honour of men like Sir Norman is questioned, then the honour of the City is questioned; and if that is doubted, then Sir Norman can spread his hands wide and point out in a sombre voice that foreign confidence in British commercial and financial integrity is undermined: 'trust and confidence is the oxygen of the City, whether it be the confidence of the investor in his stockbroker; of the broker in the jobber; the confidence of a shipowner in his insurance at Lloyd's; the confidence of a trader in a bill of exchange; or the confidence of foreign bankers in the determination of the Bank of England to maintain the value of sterling.'

On this assumption of trust reposes the whole structure of the City. Given this, the City can efficiently carry out its functions of easing the flow of goods and money, raising capital, collecting and investing the country's savings, and promoting international trade. The services which the City renders the country internally are rarely if ever questioned. Sir Norman would point out that we are reminded of them whenever we cash or write a cheque, obtain bank credit, take out an insurance policy, or invest in the industrial undertakings of the country.

·   ·   ·   ·   ·

Abroad, the City, as Mr. Thorneycroft once said of the sterling area, 'brings to us a great deal in the way of wealth, strength, and prestige'. Now, when this aspect of the City's activities is being proved quite fiercely, Sir Norman probably has some facts and figures at his finger-tips. He might claim, for example, that the City earns about £125 million pounds a year in foreign exchange—'no mean contribution to Britain's balance of payments'. His list of City contributors to this sum would include brokers' services, general merchanting activity, profits on the foreign operations of British banks, the merchant bankers' business in acceptance credits, the earnings of the Baltic Exchange, and of the insurance companies overseas. 'No other capital city can offer such a wide range of services', he will add. Sir Norman is convinced of the value of those services to the world and to Britain, and the value of his own services to Britain and the City.

He may grudgingly admit that, 'in this day and age', the City should be rather more conscious of the need to explain itself to the general public. Here, he might point to the attempts made by the Stock Exchange authorities in recent years to interest a wider public in shareholding. He would admit to their essential febrility perhaps, but at least he would claim that they were steps in the right direction; he might mention the 'new look' given to the Annual Report of the Bank of England for 1957–1958—which, incidentally, was roundly criticized by Lombard of the *Financial Times* as claiming credit for Bank policies where credit was not wholly due; and—as an example of the remarkable elasticity of the City establishment, he would point to the banking system's invasion of the hire purchase field in the summer of 1958.

Nevertheless, this last point would remind him to urge that the City must not move too fast. It is very conscious of the need for respecting tradition, it has behind it a long period of reluctance to share its secrets, and it must at all costs remain respectable. Thus, although the City's financial acumen tells it when the time has come to take advantage of hire purchase, it is not yet ready, for example, to look on the take-over bidder other than with a stare of horrified disapproval.

Having listened patiently to this recital of the virtues of Sir Norman Tullis and partners, one ventures a first protest: is there not a strong element of double-think in the City's attitude to the take-over bid technique? The City would loudly applaud the concept that the nation's capital resources should be employed to full effect and not allowed to stagnate unproductively—the very belief which is the mainspring of the take-over bidder's activities; and moreover, when the City establishment itself enters the take-over market (such as the offers of the Banks for the share capital of the largest hire-purchase companies) Nelsonian blind eyes abound. *It is, in fact, the nature of the extra-establishment people involved in take-over activity, rather than the activity itself, which offends the City fathers.*

The entry in 1958 into the hire-purchase finance stakes by the joint stock banks was one of the most extraordinary exercises by the City establishment in recent years. It is not so long since the hire-purchase finance houses were springing up and flourishing mightily outside City traditional control of any kind. For a long time the Capital Issues Committee resisted applications from the finance companies for increases in capital. The City banks courted them, proposed to them and married them in a whirlwind romance, and endowed them with a respectability which they never enjoyed before. As one irate reader of the *Financial Times* wrote to that newspaper: '. . . the Committee's frown of dis-approval on applications by finance companies for issues of capital to their own stockholders has been transformed overnight into benevolent smiles on applications for similar issues to the joint stock banks.'

He added: '. . . is there some sinister motive behind the recent spate of permitted issues to the banks? . . . it is at least possible to construe the latest moves as part of a Government design to strengthen its present stranglehold over the nation's financial affairs.'

The whole operation testified undoubtedly to the 'adaptability' of the City. After regarding hire purchase for many years as something nasty in the woodshed, the City found that the finance houses were beginning to form a secondary quasi-banking system outside its jurisdiction and control. Supremely realist, and opportunistic to the finger-tips, the City coolly corralled them in. Integrity? Tradition? Confidence? What are the real motives behind these grand words, behind the suave exteriors, beneath the bowler hats?

.   .   .   .   .

The answer was given in the evidence before the Bank Rate Leak Tribunal in the winter of 1957. The Bank Rate Tribunal led in turn to the appointment of the Radcliffe Committee to inquire into the desirability of the system by which all but four of the Bank of England's Court of Directors are part-time directors. The Bank Rate Tribunal itself observed that its 'inquiries into the dealings of Companies with which Lord Kindersley and Mr. W. J. Keswick were connected has focused attention on circumstances in which a Director of the Bank of England, who has other business interests, may find himself in a difficult and embarrassing position'. True, the Tribunal stated unequivocally that as far as directors and officials of the Bank of England were concerned, there had been no suggestion, nor any shred of evidence, that any of them improperly disclosed information about the raising of the Bank Rate. But after the dust had settled, there were still many to shake their heads and demand, like Mr. Wilson, whether, when something was known to be afoot at the Bank of England, and Lord Kindersley's colleagues at Lazards had to steer clear of him in consequence, that would 'tend to affect their decisions on other matters'?

Perhaps worse still (for the City's peace of mind), there was the impact of the very holding of a Tribunal which paraded before the public eye august City personages who spoke at times in a way which caused derision, if not stupefaction, among the vulgar. Again, Mr. Wilson summed up this aspect of the business when he said: 'One of the impressions many people have formed is the essentially amateurish way in which vital decisions affecting our whole economic well-being are taken. The old boy network, the grouse moors, and "Nigel was so depressed".'

Though many are brought to realize as they grow old that outside art, there is little that is really absolutely professional in life, the Bank Rate Tribunal nevertheless shattered a myth of professional efficiency at the centre of Britain's economic affairs. The City establishment was seen to be more amateur than has ever been supposed, cut off from the main stream of public opinion, and, even, not quite sure itself of what it was meant to be doing when it came to high matters of national policy. It was surprising to learn that City men gained their tips as to what and what not to buy from the newspapers: it was even more surprising to discover that the whole City rested on nothing more than a criss-cross system of upper-class gossip. The City, in fact, was revealed as a pompous sphinx without a secret. Mr. Andrew Shonfield, Economic Editor of the *Observer*, argued that, although the Bank of England had been nationalized there had, in fact, been virtually no change since pre-nationalization days. It maintained its old traditions—one of which was a 'tradition of secrecy', so that the City as a whole still knew little about its doings; and, at a time of crisis in the middle of September, 1957 —it had demonstrated a 'slow footed approach' and the 'absence of a prepared intellectual position'. There was still a confusion of functions between the Bank and the Treasury, with large undefined areas of responsibility. What Britain needed, Mr Shonfield concluded, was a modern Central Bank with a certain measure of independence and with professional direction. In an aside, he remarked how the public school spirit and its characteristic hierarchical organization remained extremely strong in the City.

At all this, Sir Norman Tullis and Partners were understandably aggrieved. The Tribunal, to their mind, had proved the wisdom of the City, and its righteousness, not its ineptitude and dishonesty. If anyone has been on trial at the Tribunal, it was the trouble-making left-wing politicians who regarded all City men as 'wide boys' and who were blinded by a deep and irrational class hatred for it. And then, after the Tribunal had returned a resounding verdict of not guilty, all that the Press or public for the most part did was talk of the need for reform and change! The rumbling caused by these suspicions will not be quickly ended: they have, furthermore, coincided with another debate, also prejudicial to the City, and likely to weaken further the Establishment in general. This concerns the maintenance of the Sterling Area in its present form. It first began to become heated about the time of the financial crisis in the autumn of 1957, when voices were heard arguing that Britain's obligations to the whole sterling area imposed an unnecessary strain on Britain's own balance of payments and on its people's own standard of living. The *pros* and *cons* have been set forth time and time again and are not themselves entirely relevant in this context.

However, the controversy about the Sterling Area inevitably involved the City. For one of the arguments of those who see no reason for changing the existing sterling system is that any drastic change would hinder the City, which depends on the backing of a great international currency in order to function effectively. And, as suggested above, men like Sir Norman Tullis are convinced that the efficient functioning of the City of London is essential to the economic well-being of the country.

However, it is only recently that Sir Norman has tried to calculate what exactly the City is worth to Britain in the way of earning power. The figure he might quote for the City's foreign exchange earnings we gave before as £125 million a year. But that, of course, is only one of several notoriously broad estimates, and among the highest. Another figure that has been produced is £30 million a year. In fact, as Sir Norman knows perfectly well, there just do not exist any reliable figures for the City's contribution to the balance of payments. Defenders of the City tend to put them higher than they are, while hostile critics tend to underestimate them. Mr. Shonfield reckons that 'the total of the City's merchanting and banking earnings, on the official "broad estimates", comes to £55 million'. To this can be added the earnings of 'two important activities associated with the City . . . overseas insurance business and the chartering of ships through the Baltic Exchange'. These could bring in another £60 million a year.

The relevance of these figures to the continuing debate about Sterling Area is not our concern here; nor is it feasible to consider whether foreign exchange earnings are any final criterion for the economic justification of an institution. The figures, however, are relevant in that they illustrate both the vagueness that surrounds much of the City's activities—and, *a fortiori*, the mystery surrounding the City establishment. In this context, the way they have been bandied about recently with a certain amount of acerbity, has illustrated the increasingly critical attitude being adopted towards the shibboleths of the City by the Press and the public.

Of course, it can be pleaded that the City is not a single concern which could—even if it wanted to—present an annual statement. After all, there is no single authority for the City of London competent and duty-bound to inform the public what the City contributes to the country's overseas earnings. The Bank of England, where it is concerned with the balance of payments, is concerned as a national, not a City, institution. One could as well take it to task for not publishing the contribution made to Britain's balance of payments by the Middle East oil companies, as for not publishing that made by the City. Both calculations are extremely difficult to make. It is argued also that the confidence system practised by the City, moreover, creates intangible assets which are incapable of evaluation. If, hypothetically, the City were able to present a balance sheet, who would be bold enough to calculate an entry for goodwill? In short, one cannot be moralistic about this matter; one can, however, suggest strongly that more information be made public by the authorities: so that the public, and publicists, can make up their mind for themselves.

How much the public at large, in truth, thinks about the City in relation to the economy of the country and its social evolution is anyone's guess, for it is undoubtedly thoroughly ignorant about the City's mechanism. What little public knowledge exists is limited to a vague awareness of what goes on at the Stock Exchange, together with an appreciation of City traditions and pageantry. The City can claim that its job is basically to create wealth, and that if the general public is ignorant of how it does this, the general public itself—or the Government—is to blame. On the other hand, it can be argued with greater force that City leaders, like industrial leaders, have a positive duty to foster knowledge of their activities whenever possible, and that, in this, they are failing quite lamentably. It can also be argued that if the City goes on assuming that it has no need to justify its existence to the public—which does not, incidentally, necessarily accept the economic philosophy on which the City is based—the public will be totally apathetic about its fate when subjected to calculatedly hostile political pressures.

Inevitably, I have fallen into the trap of talking about the City as if it were a corporate entity. There are about half a million people working in the square mile of the City, which is almost deserted by night. As we have already said, it can be assumed that most of the City workers are conservative in sentiment, but, of course, comparatively few of them are much more enlightened than the public at large about the organization and functions of the City, and even fewer come near to the centres of power. The very few, the *élite*, are not so much members of the Establishment because they have succeeded in the City; they have succeeded in the City because they are members of the Establishment.

. . . . . .

It can be assumed that the Establishment as a whole draws a good deal of its wealth and authority from its commercial section in the City. It would be invidious to examine the earnings of the City gods; but it is not offensive to consider the actual economic power in their hands.

Here again English dislike of definition makes the task difficult. Nonetheless there are some indications available to us. In simple fashion, for example, one may recall that a number of important City people are known to have the ear of the Governor of the Bank of England. Indeed, the very system of having part-time directors of the Bank of England is usually justified by the desirability of framing official policy with an awareness of 'what the City is thinking'. But men who take advice are influenced by that advice, sometimes, perhaps, unduly so; this is especially likely when the seeker of advice is of the same social class and background as the men who tender it. In the case of the Bank of England we have, to put it mildly, the possibility of schizophrenia, given its unique relationship with the City and its unique role of custodian of the country's economic interests. There must be at least a chance that, on occasion, the eagle should prove to have two heads. But how much power does the Bank of England in fact possess?

Again, we walk into a fog. On the one hand, the Chancellor of the Exchequer will have the last word if there is a direct clash between his will and that of the Governor's. On the other, although severe differences of opinion between Bank and Treasury officials are not uncommon, direct clashes of will are; and if the policy to be followed is arguable, the Chancellor is likely to listen carefully to a Governor who can claim the support of influential City opinion, when he is either asked for advice on, or initiates, a particular course of action. Exact areas of responsibility have never been delineated. The Chancellor's word may be law in the last resort; but in the last resort, the Governor can always say that if something is done of which he does not approve—or something is not done which he recommends—the Bank will not be responsible for the consequences. This could be a considerable threat.

It seems, however, that the Bank is usually left a free hand in certain spheres, while the Treasury makes the running in others; for example, it seems likely that during recent years the Bank has had the bigger influence on matters of internal monetary policy

—such as the level of the Bank Rate—while Treasury officials have kept tight policy control over foreign exchange matters.

However this may be, the Bank of England is an immensely powerful institution, the Governor is a very powerful man, and both are open to influence, albeit perhaps wholesome influence, by the City establishment.

Through its influence on the Chancellor and through its own direct responsibility for the national economy, the Bank exerts a considerable influence on all our lives. The top ranks of the Bank's hierarchy are part of the City establishment, influenced by and in turn influencing it. The Bank's control over interest rates and the money supply extends its influence into every branch of industry, commerce and, indeed, private life. That is known and obvious; but in mentioning it it is worth adding that although the Bank possesses wide legal powers in these matters, it dislikes any show of coercion, relying instead—in typical Establishment fashion—on the subtler methods of persuasion and a show of wise authority.

The joint stock banks, the Big Five and the Little Six, subordinate to the Bank of England in matters affecting national monetary policy, themselves, of course, exercise direct power through their immense credit resources in the country at large and, again, through their personal connections in the City. Add to all this the great wealth of the merchant banks and their economic influence; add also the resources of the great insurance companies with their international ramifications, and a complex of wealth, prestige, authority and power is revealed, all the more formidable because of its geographical concentration, and the mutual sympathies of the men who ultimately control it.

And there is, moreover, the influence exercised by the City establishment in spheres other than its own economic one, precisely because its opinions are backed by the wealth and prestige of the whole City. This extends to the Press, the arts, the universities, politics and the Civil Service. Power, and the capacity to influence, tends to agglomerate and spread far outside the limited territories over which it was originally designed to rule.

· · · · ·

Relations between the Press and the City are confused, intricate and lively. The once popular Socialist image of a capitalist Press serving the lords of the Establishment is remote from the truth. Of course, there is a section of the Press strongly favoured by Government circles. For example, during last year's acute financial crisis, the then Chancellor, in order to get co-operation from the newspapers, saw representatives of the *Financial Times*, the *Economist*, *The Times*, the *News Chronicle*, the *Daily Telegraph*, Reuters, and the *Manchester Guardian*. It could be argued that he was electing to see what he considered to be the more responsible section of the Press, not that with which there were necessarily mutual political sympathies. But that is not the point. The crucial point is that all the pressmen (who included a peer and a baronet) whom he saw, have far easier access to the Political establishment than, with certain exceptions, to the City establishment.

In fact, although there are intimate ties between various printing houses and newspaper chains and the City, it is notable that there have been a fair number of Press lords with backgrounds and opinions considered outrageous by the City establishment; that journalists, generally speaking, tend to despise it, especially when having to record the antics of its socialite fringe; that it is in the very financial columns of the Press that astringent criticism of City obscurity and myth is most apparent.

The independence of the Press *vis-a-vis* the City establishment is in fact surprising. Consider, for instance, the *Financial Times*. Under the chairmanship of Lord Bracken that newspaper, although profoundly anti-socialist and occasionally tolerating facetious attacks on the Labour Party, acquired an international reputation for accurate and impartial reporting and comparatively unbiased comment. Certainly, whatever its political leanings, it showed no sycophancy as far as the City establishment was concerned, and in its columns was—and is—to be found some of the most acute criticism of the City and of Conservative economic policies which appears anywhere in the British Press. The frequency with which the *Financial Times* is quoted in debate by Labour M.P.s gives perhaps an indication of this remarkable independence of outlook.

The *Financial Times* acquired very close links with the Establishment when, in 1957, ownership was acquired by S. Pearson Industries, one of a group of companies controlled by the Pearson Family Trust, of which Lord Cowdray (Eton and Christ Church, Oxford) is chairman. On its board are Lord

Drogheda (Eton and Trinity College, Cambridge) and Lord Poole (Eton and Christ Church, Oxford), a member of Lloyd's, and Chairman of the Conservative Party from 1955–57. Establishment of the Establishment, via polo, Covent Garden and the Conservative Party respectively, this *troika* of old Etonian peers imposes no gag on their journal's occasional criticisms of City institutions and Conservative Government economic policy.

In the Beaverbrook Press, we find economic and financial attitudes, which often border on the ridiculous, but never vary in their readiness to mock, affront and lecture the City of London. Its financial columns are generally on the side, at one and the same time, of the adventurous financier and the small investor; it abhors above all, the stuffy and reticent—its own adjectives are 'toffee-nosed' and 'high-hat'—as descriptive attitudes of the City fathers. When the banks go into hire-purchase it splashes the news gaily, as if reporting nude bathing in the Serpentine by distinguished Belgravia hostesses.

The City columns in the Press, by and large, are a thorn in the side of the City establishment rather than a public relations service for it. The staid *Times*, the more politically conscious *Mail*, *Chronicle* and *Telegraph*, though basically fond of the City establishment, are above all anxious to lighten the darkness of their readers by increasing public understanding of the City's mysteries. The *Daily Herald* sports a reasonably sensible but, one fears, very unread column; while the *Daily Mirror*, which is to the *lumpen proletariat* what the *Daily Express* is to the *lumpen bourgeoisie*, realizes that as far as the masses are concerned, the City—sexual and financial scandals apart—is not yet good copy. *Mirror* readers, unwooed by the City are, in turn, basically indifferent to it.

On examination, therefore, we find that the newspapers with the biggest circulations amounting to nearly 10 million copies each day in total, the *Mirror* and the *Express*, are indifferent and hostile, respectively, towards the City. The concept of a sycophantic Press, devoted to buttressing the supports of the City system, is a ludicrous one.

．　　　．　　　．　　　．　　　．

Our Sir Norman Tullis might well comment that the concentration of power and influence in the hands of very few men is in

no way reprehensible; that it is natural enough for men at the top
in any kind of activity to form a cohesive group, and to maintain
close relations with other groups of equal stature. And is the ruling
group of the City after all so cohesive? Cannot anyone coming to
the City (and Dick Whittington is one of the City's proudest
traditions) find his fortune there, and climb into the ranks of the
so-called Establishment?

It seems undeniable that although the occasional outsider may
acquire wealth in the City through merchanting or trading of some
kind or another his chances in the main City institutions—the
insurance companies and Lloyd's, the head offices of the banks,
the Bank of England itself—are slender unless he is backed by
respectable inherited wealth and a suitable education.

The importance of the Stock Exchange in the power complex
can easily be exaggerated. Stockbrokers are, in fact, very much
more aides-de-camp to the City gods, than policy makers within
the context of the City establishment. They are for the most part
a body of sound and reliable people possessed of all the necessary
qualities of the City man. But few stockbrokers ever exercise anything but marginal power in the golden mile. For this reason,
perhaps, membership of the London Stock Exchange can be
aspired to by those who do not possess great wealth or influence.
For the most part intelligent but unintellectual, thoughtful but
unimaginative, stockbrokers are a most unjustly maligned section
of the City community. Entry in their ranks is, contrary to popular
belief, open to all, regardless of wealth, background or education.
The only bar which is imposed is not a class, but a sex, bar.
Women may have obtained a foothold in the upper reaches of
Westminster, but not for many a long summer will a female voice
be heard transacting business on the floor of the London Stock
Exchange.

Lloyd's is considered with very much more reason a hot-
house of privilege. (The new building that houses it has baths for
those who toil within—a remarkable City innovation.) The 3,000
or so underwriting members, operating as 'private and particular'
persons in syndicates, but without limited liability, cannot even
start their career without substantial wealth, both to meet possible
liabilities, and to provide the heavy deposit of solid securities
which is a *sine qua non* of their membership. But here again,
although salaried (and very highly salaried) managers provide

much of the technical expertise, it is an essential part of the confidence system that names denoting solid wealth—and the integrity that the possession of great wealth usually ensures—should be roped into the City network.

. . . . .

The Stock Exchange and Lloyd's are unique institutions, and their worst enemies have never been able to impugn seriously either their integrity or the general efficiency of their mechanisms.

Let us look at the Bank of England and the Big Five banks, more rightly comparable with other institutions. Here, high executive and managerial positions can be aspired to but infrequently by capable men starting from scratch. On the Court of Directors of the Bank of England, for instance, is one who was educated at Chalfont St. Giles Council School, but the few who did not learn their Latin and Greek at the ancestral seats of education are exceptional. The Governor of the Bank of England was educated at Eton and King's College, Cambridge; two others on the Court were educated at Marlborough and Corpus Christi, Cambridge; another was educated at Eton and Sandhurst; two others at Eton and Trinity, Cambridge; another at Eton; another at Wellington; another at Winchester and Trinity, Cambridge; another at Eton and Trinity, Oxford; another at Rugby and Magdalene, Cambridge; another at Rugby and Trinity, Oxford; another at Winchester.

In the Big Five, Viscount Monckton of Brenchley (Harrow and Balliol), is chairman of the Midland Bank; he is also the chairman of the Iraq Petroleum Company. He represents the incursion into the City establishment of those top-level lawyers who, free to choose between high judicial or political office on the one hand, or boardroom posts in the banks and oil companies on the other, have not hesitated to choose the latter. On a reasoned comparison of the real power (not to mention the financial rewards which could only be of marginal importance to them) which they might expect to exercise, there can be little doubt that their choice was a correct one. Talents that in former days were rewarded in the Army, the Church and the Law are more than ever now finding their home in the City.

There is, for instance, an array of military talent in the boardrooms of the Big Five which might have justifiably terrified

F

Britain's enemies in the field, but must surely have the opposite effect on the acute men of Zurich, whose damaging guerilla warfare on sterling forms a major threat to Britain's economic stability.

The chairman of the National Provincial Bank was educated at Eton and Magdalen, Oxford; the chairman of the Westminster Bank at Eton and Trinity, Cambridge; the chairman of Barclays at Winchester. (Only one of the Big Five banks even recognizes the National Union of Bank Employees to which a large proportion of their staffs belong. The exception, Barclays Bank, which took the not very dreadful step of granting recognition to the union seventeen years ago, dropped a bombshell in the banking world in 1958 when it appointed a woman manager of an important London branch.)

The list of educational privilege can be extended indefinitely. Perhaps we may extend to the City rulers the attitude of mind which Stanley Baldwin, with characteristic frankness, portrayed in the political sphere, when he said: "When the call came to me to form a Government, one of my first thoughts was that it should be a Government of which Harrow should not be ashamed. I remembered how, in previous Governments, there had been four or perhaps five Harrovians—and I determined to have six!"

Lord Kindersley, a prototype City establishment figure, is an old Etonian on the Court of Directors of the Bank of England. He is also, *inter alia*, chairman of Lazards, the great merchant bankers, Governor of the Royal Exchange Assurance Company, and chairman of Rolls-Royce. He is clearly one of the most powerful men in the City, and, therefore, in the country. But until the Bank Rate Tribunal it is extremely doubtful if his name would have been known to anything more than a tiny section of the population. He, Sir Norman Tullis, and a few others have enjoyed for generations power without responsibility—except for their innate *sense* of responsibility to the City and the country, which is no more justifiable than was Hitler's sense that he was expressive of the common national will. This great feeling of responsibility has in fact served the country well in the nineteenth century, but in recent times—even from those who recognize this fact—there has been a clamouring from without for the curtailment of the City's massive power over the life of the nation.

The City, like, for instance, the Foreign Office, is an essentially undemocratic complex of forces in a politically democratic society. The invasion of its privacy and its privilege might easily impair its machinery; if this were to happen the nation would certainly be a net loser. But by an over-zealous guarding of its powers, it is helping to create forces outside which question and threaten its very existence as at present constituted.

The random instances of educational advantage given above serve merely to indicate a characteristic which the City establishment, or many members of it, share with the Establishment generally. That many chairmen in the City should have had the same sort of education is not in the least surprising; that this education should be of the grander sort is equally to be expected; chairmen, able and talented as many of them are, are also chosen for their value as adornment, because they are agreeable people to talk to, and because they share the prejudices of their City colleagues.

.   .   .   .   .

Lord Pakenham (Eton and New College, Oxford), chairman of the National Bank and a socialist who, quite exceptionally, may fairly be described as a member of the City establishment, wrote in the *Daily Telegraph* that 'Socialist politicians make a mistake if they regard the average boardroom as a conscious extension of the Conservative party'. Here, we may presume, the key word was 'conscious'. Most people in the City who have some salaried position are in fact probably rather more irrationally anti-socialist than the City establishment itself. Generally speaking, from the amount of anti-socialist propaganda they indulge in, industrialists as a class tend to be far more vehemently anti-socialist than the City establishment. Self-made men, and men who have climbed fairly high through (but not to the top of) the capitalist system, tend to be more ferocious defenders of unlimited free enterprise than those who actually run the system from above. The City establishment is too conscious of its entrenched power and too aware of its national responsibilities, to be foolishly partisan in the political game. And, after all, although a Labour Party thoroughly bent on achieving a socialist society would wreck the City as it is today, the damage to the commodity markets and the Stock Exchange, where the Establishment is, if not poorly represented, at least politically and economically weak, would, for example, be greatest. Whilst the outer periphery might suffer, the damage to the hierarchy of the Banks and the Bank of England, the insurance companies and Lloyd's would almost certainly be least. The Bank of England was nationalized by an exuberant Labour Government very soon after the end of the war; a Rip Van Winkle at the Parker Tribunal might reasonably have assumed that the Act of Nationalization had been repealed. *Plus ça change.* . . .

The City establishment, however, if not fanatically and openly Conservative, is certainly conservative by instinct and training to an extent that cuts it off from the life of the nation in a much more deep-rooted way than political bias alone could ensure. Its public school standards of conduct; its upper-class standard of life, its sports and its formalities; even its assumption that the City is of vital importance to the economic well-being of the country and that free markets are inevitably the best markets, mean that it lives in a world, physically and mentally, apart from the world of the vast majority of the population. This, when the City is undoubtedly economically very powerful indeed, is certainly dangerous. There is nothing to parallel the situation (with the possible exception of Russia) in any other advanced industrial country.

. . . . .

Earlier on, we inferred that the split between the Labour Party and the City was fundamentally a split between socialism and the Establishment. As it happens, the most virulent hostility towards the City on the part of Labour Party members comes uniformly from those who least understand its workings; who go bald-headed for shady trading deals, the activities of predatory take-over experts, for the immorality of slick share dealing. The City establishment, which shrinks in even greater horror from such abuses, emerges absolutely unscratched from such a confused battle. If we think of the social rather than the economic characteristics of the City, we must surely conclude that the real gulf is between democratic socialism and the City establishment, rather than between the Labour Party and the City as a whole.

Neither the ill-informed, and often ridiculous, criticism with which its enemies assail it on the one hand, nor the stern unbending refusal of the City establishment to compromise with 'lesser breeds without the law' on the other, help towards a sane solution of a major social and economic problem. The power of the City in the life of a nation is enormous, and on the whole, although oligarchically controlled, it is not blatantly abused. But it remains important that there should be close scrutiny of the use of great power in any shape or form; and that aspiration should be open to talent from whatever class or education. The seats of power should not be the perquisite of a small nepotic patrician minority.

APPENDIX:
THE TOP FOUR HUNDRED

(The pluralists of the city, with their other directorates)

MERCHANT BANKERS

LAZARDS

LORD KINDERSLEY: Bank of England, Bank of London & South America, Royal Exchange (Dr.), Rolls-Royce (Ch.), British Match.

LORD BRAND: Lloyds Bank, *The Times*.

HON. T. H. BRAND: Lloyd's, Employers Liability, Borax.

A. D. MARRIS: Barclays Bank, Commercial Union Ass., P. & O., Wm. Cory.

P. HORSFALL: Phoenix Ass., English Electric.

D. MEINERZHAGEN: Mercantile Credit, W. T. Henley.

G. GODFREY PHILIPS: Equity & Law Life, B.S.A., English Electric.

J. MACARTNEY FILGATE: Tube Investments, Eagle Oil.

HON. D. F. BRAND: Eng., Scot. & Aust. Bank, Aust. Mercantile, Comm. Union Ass.

HAMBROS

SIR CHAS. HAMBRO: Bank of England, Provident & Mutual Life, Cable & Wireless.

J. H. HAMBRO: John Dickinson.

J. O. HAMBRO: Phoenix Ass., Consolidated Mines Selection.

R. D. HAMBRO (Ch.): London Ass. (Gov.).

LORD GLENCONNER: National Mortgage Bank of N.Z. (Ch.), Northern Ass. (Ch.), I.C.I.

SIR ERNEST OPPENHEIMER: Barclays D.C.O., De Beers, Anglo-American Corp.

A. J. H. SMITH: British Metal Corp.

G. L. D'ABO: Covent Gdn. Properties, Diamond Dev.

H. N. SPORBORG: Alliance Ass., Atlas Ins.

LORD ASTOR OF HEVER: Phoenix Ass., London Guarantee & Acc. Ins.

C. E. A. HAMBRO: Royal Exchange Ass.

MORGAN GRENFELL

LORD BICESTER: Bank of England, Mercantile Bank of India, Yule Catto, A.E.I., Vickers, Shell.

SIR GEO. ERSKINE: Guest, Keen & Nettlefold, Union Castle, British Commonwealth Shipping, Harrods.

W. W. H. HILL-WOOD: Commercial Union Ass., British Celanese.

LORD RENNELL OF RODD: National Bank of Australia, Planet, Sun, Sun Life Ins. (J.Ch.), B.O.A.C.

J. E. H. COLLINS: Royal Exchange, Hudson's Bay.

VISCT. HARCOURT: Greshams', Legal & General Ins.

PHILLIP HILL, HIGGINSON

H. C. DRAYTON: Midland Bank, Eagle Star Ins., British Electric Traction (Ch.), Antofagasta Rlwy., Ashanti Gold.

K. H. PRESTON: Midland Bank, Platt Bros. (Ch.), W. & T. Avery, Export Credits Advisory Council.

W. M. CODRINGTON: Sun, Sun Life Ins., Rank Org., Powell Duffryn, Antofagasta Rlwy.

H. A. MEREDITH: Beecham Gp., Hawker Siddeley, Strong & Co.

H. R. MOORE: Rank Org., Covent Gdn. Properties.

J. R. COLVILLE: Ottoman Bank, Eagle Star, Rio Tinto.

D. E. WEBB: Phoenix Ass., Beecham Gp.

K. A. KEITH: Eagle Star Ins., Beecham Group, United Draperies.

R. E. F. DE TRAFFORD: Wm. Deacon's Bank, Atlas Ass.

BENSON & LONSDALE

C. E. BENSON: Lloyds Bank, Montagu Burton.

LORD ROCKLEY: Nat. Provincial Bank, Ilford, Schweppes.

SIR MARK TURNER: Mercantile Credit (Ch.), Commercial Union Ass., Calico Printers Ass., Brit. Home Stores, Rio Tinto, Tanganyika Concessions.

R. F. MEDLICOTT: Barclays D.C.O., Central Mining & Invest.

G. P. S. McPHERSON: British & French Bank, Standard Life Ass.

D. L. P. OPPÉ: Anglo-Chinese Finance (Ch.), Maple, Cementation, British Sulphur (Ch.).

FLEMING

P. FLEMING (Ch.): Scottish Amicable Ins.

R. E. FLEMING: Barclays Bank (& D.C.O.), London Ass., Commonwealth Development Corp.

M. F. BERRY: Westminster Bank, Metropolitan Life & London Life Ins., Capital Issues Committee.

D. J. Robarts: Nat. Provincial Bank (Ch.), Australia and N.Z. Bank, Sun, Sun Life Ins., Coutts Bank, Yorkshire Penny Bank, Union Discount Bank, I.C.I.

G. J. Jamieson: Sun, Sun Life Ins., London Tin Corp. -

H. N. Money-Coutts: Mercantile & General Reinsurance.

DE STEIN'S

Sir Edward de Stein (Ch.): Gallaher, E.M.I.

G. W. ff Dawnay: Barclays, Guardian Ass., E.M.I., Dalgety (DCh.).

Hon. David Bowes Lyon: Martins Bank, Nat. Discount Bank, Cunard, Dunlop, *The Times*, Royal Exchange Ass.

M. R. Norman: Wm. Deacon's Bank, Brit. Bank of the M.E., Union Discount Bank, Gallaher, Staveley Coal & Iron, Wiggins Teape.

GIBBS

Lord Aldenham: Westminster Bank (Ch.), Yorkshire Penny Bank, Eng., Scot. & Aust. Bank, Commercial Union Ass., British Match Corp.

Sir G. C. Gibbs: Barclays D.C.O. (DCh.), Australia and N.Z. Bank, Union Discount Bank, Australian Mutual Provident Ins., Export Credit Advisory Council.

H. K. Goschen: London Life, Metropolitan Life Ass., Mercantile & General Reinsurance, Rubber Holdings.

Earl of Ranfurly: Colonial Mutual Life Ins., Overseas Holdings, Ltd.

BARINGS

Earl of Cromer: Royal Ins., Liverpool, London & Globe Ins., Lewis's Investment Trust, *Daily Mail*.

Lord Ashburton: Alliance Ass., Pressed Steel Co.

J. G. Philimore: North British, Fine Art & General Ins., Liebig, Oxo, W. H. Smith, Brazilian Traction.

A. H. Cannwarth: Equity & Law Life Ins.

SCHRODERS

H. W. B. Schroder (Ch.): Lima Light & Power.

A. Abel Smith: Provident Mutual Life Ins., Pressed Steel Co.

G. W. H. Richardson: Legal & General Ins., Head Wrightson, Westinghouse Brake.

Hon. A. L. Hood: A.E.I., Wimpey, Blaw Knox.

H. F. Tiarks: Joseph Lucas, Pressed Steel, Antofagasta Rlwy.

J. Backhouse: Nat. Provident Institute for Mutual Life, Sena Sugar Estates.

S. JAPHET

SIR H. NUTCOMBE HUME: Charterhouse Investment, Edmundson's Electric (Ch.), Curry's (Ch.), Colonial Development Corp., National Film Finance Corp. (Ch.).

SIR ARTHUR MORSE: Hong Kong & Shanghai Bank, Bowmakers (Ch.).

J. E. McNISH: Charterhouse Investment, Platt Bros., etc.

E. H. OWEN: Charterhouse Investment, Grindlay's Bank.

C. M. RAIT: Charterhouse, National Bank, N. African Mining.

HELBERT WAGG

W. LIONEL FRASER (Ch.): Atlas Ins. (DCh.), Babcock & Wilcox (Ch.), Thos. Tilling (Ch.).

C. H. VILLIERS: Banque Belge, Standard Bank of S. Africa, Sun, Sun Life Ins., United Premium Oil & Cake.

A. PALACHE: British Sugar Corp., Commercial Plastics, Revertas.

A. RUSSELL: District Bank, Alexander's Discount Bank, I.B.M. (U.K.).

HON. W. B. L. BARRINGTON: Gresham Fire (Ch.), Legal & General Ins. (Ch.).

A. C. G. PONSONBY: Employers Liability Ins.

R. HOLLAND: Commercial Union Ass.

M. VEREY: Northern Ass., Australian Mercantile, Land & Finance.

GRAY, DAWES & McNEILL

EARL OF INCHCAPE: Nat. Provincial Bank, Chartered Bank, Bank of West Africa, P. & O., Alex. Shanks (Ch.), Upper Assam Tea, etc.

SIR WM. CURRIE: Wm. Deacon's Bank (DCh.), Royal Bank of Scotland, Marine, Marine & General Ins., P. & O., Wm. Cory, Orient Steam Navigation, etc., Suez Canal Co.

GUINNESS & MAHON

H. E. GUINNESS: Union Ass. (Irish), Dunlop, W. & R. Jacob.

H. S. H. GUINNESS: Provincial Bank of Ireland, National Discount Bank, Commercial Banking Co. of Sydney.

SIR GEO. MAHON: Mercantile Credit Co., Cerebos.

D. R. SCHOLEY: Sphere Ins. (Ch.), Orion Ins. (DCh.).

J. E. A. R. GUINNESS: Provident Mutual Life Ins.

MATHESONS

W. JOHNSTONE KESWICK: Bank of England, Alliance Ass., B.P., Hudson's Bay Co.

J. H. KESWICK: Martins Bank, Hong Kong & Shanghai Bank, Thistle Ins., Malayan Para Rubber, etc.

YULE, CATTO

SIR ALEX AIKMAN: Guardian Ass., Dunlop, E.M.I.
SIR J. H. S. RICHARDSON: Chartered Bank, Goodlass, Wall & Lead.
SIR ALEXANDER SIM: W. T. Henley.
SIR KEN MEALING: Mercantile Bank of India (Ch.), Eastern Ins. &
Reinsurance (Ch.), Hoogly Co., Ultramar.

D'ERLANGERS

LEO D'ERLANGER: British S. Africa Co., Harrods, Almin.
GERARD D'ERLANGER: Provident Mutual Ins., John Mackintosh,
B.O.A.C.
A. O. BLUTH: Vickers, Oldings (Ch.).

ROTHSCHILD

LORD ROTHSCHILD: Alliance Ass., Anglo-American Corp., Rio Tinto,
Central Mining & Investment.
N. M. ROTHSCHILD: Ditto.

SAMUELS

HON. P. M. SAMUEL: Shell, Anglo-Saxon Petrol.
VISCT. BEARSTEAD: Alliance Ass.
R. G. E. JARVIS: Lloyds, Marine & General Ins.

BALFOUR, WILLIAMSON

HON. GERALD WILLIAMSON: British & Foreign Marine Ins., Lobitos
Oilfields, Rio de Janeiro Flourmills.
A. E. GRIEVE: English China Clays, Olympic Portland Cement.

REA BROS.

SIR WILFRED AYRE: Lloyds Bank, United Dominion Trust.

S. G. WARBURG

G. E. COKE: U.K. Temperance & General Provident Ins., Rio Tinto
(Ch.).
SIR ANDREW McFADYEAN: Commercial Plastics (Ch.), Rubber &
Timber companies.

STERNS

SIR A. G. STERN: Midland Bank, Ottoman Bank, Clydesdale & North
Scottish Bank.

KLEINWORT

C. H. KLEINWORT: North British Gp. of Insurance Cos. (Ch.).

SASSOON

DEREK FITZGERALD: Barclays D.C.O.
DESMOND FITZGERALD: Vere Engineering, International Plastics.

ARBUTHNOT LATHAM

J. F. PRIDEAUX: Westminster Bank & Foreign Bank, Australian Mercantile Land & Finance, Bank of N.S. Wales.
R. ABEL SMITH (Ch.): Anglo-American Debenture Corp.

BRANDTS

W. A. BRANDT (Ch.): London Ass. (Dep. Gov.).

OLD BROAD ST. SECURITIES

J. GIBSON JARVIE: United Dominions Trust, Carplant.

GRINDLAYS

SIR TOBY LOS: General Electric, John Brown, Dorman Long, Dowsett Holdings.
F.M. SIR CLAUDE AUCHINLECK: Dowsett Holdings.

COUTTS

S. J. L. EGERTON (Ch.): Nat. Provincial Bank, Phoenix Ass.
LORD CLITHEROE: Nat. Provincial Bank, Tube Investments, John Brown, Finance Corp. for Industry, Borax.
LORD LATYMER: Nat. Provincial Bank, Ottoman Bank, Public Works Loan Board.
HON. A. B. MONEY-COUTTS: Imperial Tobacco.
J. L. E. SMITH: Ottoman Bank, Royal Exchange Ass.

COMMERCIAL BANKERS

DISTRICT

SIR THOMAS BARLOW (Ch.): Barlow & Jones, Capital Issues Committee.
SIR WALTER SHEPHERD: Liverpool, London & Globe, Turner & Newall (Ch.), African, Canadian & Rhodesian Asbestos Companies.
SIR ALAN TOD: Royal, Liverpool, London & Globe Ins., Cunard, Lancs Cotton Corp., Elder Dempster.

EARL PEEL: Sea Insurance, Lancs Steel Corp., Jas. Williamson.

R. F. SUMMERS: Royal, Liverpool, London & Globe Ins., John Summers, United Steel, B.T.C. (Midlands Bd.).

ALF. WHITTLE: Wallpaper Mfg. Co. (Ch.), John Dickinson.

SIR ROBT. BURROWS: Alliance Ass., Yorkshire Penny Bank.

H. P. BIBBY: J. Bibby (Ch.).

LIEUT.-COL. T. M. BROOKS (DCh.): Horrocks Crewdson.

DUKE OF DEVONSHIRE: Alliance Ass.

NATIONAL PROVINCIAL

SIR FREDK. LEITH-ROSS (DCh.): National Discount Bank, Standard Bank of S. Africa, Babcock & Wilcox.

LORD ABERCONWAY: Hoare Bros., London Ass., Nat. Provident Institution, John Brown (Ch.), Firth, Brown.

SIR D. FORSYTH ANDERSON: Bank of Australia & N.Z., P. & O. (DCh.).

SIR ALEXANDER CADOGAN: Phoenix Ass., Suez Canal (Govt. Dir.).

S. P. CHAMBERS: Royal, Liverpool, London & Globe, I.C.I. (DCh.), N.C.B.

SIR P. J. GRIGG: Prudential, Distillers, Imperial Tobacco, Bass.

O. J. PHILIPSON: N. British & Mercantile Ins., Parsons (Ch.), Richardson, Westgarth (Ch.).

LORD STRATHALMOND: Burmah Oil.

L. J. WILLIAMS: Ranks the Millers.

EARL OF SELBORNE: N. British & Mercantile Ins., Boots, Union Minière, Tanganyika Concessions, Benguela Rlwy.

DESMOND ABEL SMITH: Bank of N.S. Wales, Equitable Life Ins., B.P., Dalgety, Borax.

SIR ROWLAND SMITH: Zürich Ins., Ford Motors, U.K. Atomic Energy Authority.

SIR IVAN STEDEFORD: Atlas Ins., Tube Investments (Ch.).

F. G. ROBINSON: E. S. A. Robinson.

E. R. COURAGE: Barclay Courage.

LLOYDS

SIR OLIVER FRANKS (Ch.): Bank of London & S. America, National Bank of Scotland, Friends Provident & Century Ins.

SIR JEREMY RAISMAN (DCh.): Alliance Ass., Glaxo, Public Works Loan Board.

HAROLD PEAKE (VCh.): Bank of London & S. America, National Bank of Scotland, Bank of Australasia (Ch.), London Ass., Steel Co. of Wales, Rolls-Royce.

A. H. ENSOR (VCh.): Bank of London & S. America, National Bank of N.Z., Legal & General Ins., Nat. Cash Register.

SIR E. C. BACON: British Sugar Corp., B.T.C. (E. Region).
LORD BALFOUR OF BURLEIGH: Nat. Bank of Scotland, Nat. Bank of N.Z.,
Yorkshire Penny Bank, Standard Bank of S. Africa, Alexanders
Discount Bank.
LORD ROWALLAN: Nat. Bank of Scotland (Gov.).
SIR ERIC VANSITTART BOWATER: Alliance Ass., Bowater Paper Corp.
(Ch.).
SIR EGBERT CADBURY: British Cocoa & Chocolate, Daily News.
VISCOUNT DE L'ISLE: Phoenix Ass., British Match Corp., Barclay
Courage, Schweppes.
SIR GEO. LEGH JONES: Shell (DCh.), B.P., Canadian Eagle (Ch.),
Anglo-Saxon Oil (Ch.).
SIR ERNEST LEVER: Richard Thomas & Baldwins (Ch.), African Metal
Corp.
LORD LUKE: Bank of London & S. America, Nat. Provident Inst.,
I.B.M., Bovril (Ch.), Virol, Australian Mercantile Land & Finance,
Ashanti Gold, Santa Fé Land.
SIR GEORGE HORATIO NELSON: English Electric (Ch.), Napier, Marconi,
Vulcan.
K. S. PEACOCK: Guest, Keen & Nettlefold, Steel Co. of Wales, United
Steel.
VISCT. RIDLEY: Yorkshire Ins., Consett Iron, Head Wrightson, Export
Credits Advisory Cttee.
L. B. ROBINSON: Australian Mutual Provident, Broken Hill (Ch.),
Consolidated Zinc (Ch.), Imperial Smelting (Ch.).
VISCT. RUNCIMAN: Runciman (Ch.), P. & O., United Molasses, Anchor
Line.
SIR REG. VERDON SMITH: Employers Liability Ins., Bristol Aeroplane
(Ch.), Babcock & Wilcox.
VISCT. BLEDISLOE: Australian Mutual Provident, P. & O.
H. L. R. MATTHEWS: Sea Ins., Abbey National Bldng., Maples, Crosse
& Blackwell.
D. M. OPPENHEIM: British American Tobacco.
A. B. WARING: Joseph Lucas (Ch.), C.A.V. (Ch.), Rotax (Ch.).
J. C. TAYLOR (Liverpool Board): Sea Ins., Cunard.
EARL OF SCARBROUGH: Standard Bank of S. Africa.
SIR JAS. TURNER: Avon Ins., National Farmers Union, Dollar Exports
Council.
E. WHITLEY-JONES: Bank of West Africa.

WESTMINSTER

D. A. STIRLING (DCh.): London Life, Mercantile & Gen. Ins.

S. G. GATES (DCh.): Bank of West Africa, National Provident Institution, Sheepbridge Engineering, Tecalemit.

SIR AUSTIN ANDERSON: P. & O., Orient.

J. A. F. BINNY: Hong Kong & Shanghai Bank, Mercantile & Gen. Ins., Assoc. Portland Cement (VCh.), Alpha Cement.

A. G. CLIFTON BROWN: Bank of N.S. Wales, Royal Exchange Ass.

EARL OF DUDLEY: Phoenix Ass., Steel Co. of Wales, W. & T. Avery.

F. E. HARMER: Bank of N.Z., London Life, Metropolitan Life, Assoc. Mutual Ins., P. & O. (DCh.), Wm. Cory, N.Z. Shipping (Ch.), B.P. (Govt. Director).

SIR ARTHUR FFORDE: Equity & Law Life Ins.

SIR WALTER BENTON-JONES: United Steel (Ch.), John Summers, Stewart & Lloyds, British Wagon.

VISCT. LEATHERS: Wm. Cory (Ch.), E.A.R.A.

MALCOLM McDOUGALL: Scottish Mutual Ins., J. & P. Coates.

SIR ERIC MIEVILLE: Silvertown Rubber (Ch.), United Premier Oil & Cake (Ch.), London Tin Corp.

D. L. POLLOCK: Legal & General Ins., Vickers, S. Pearson.

D. V. PHELPS: Pilkingtons, Chance Glass (Ch.).

MARQUESS OF SALISBURY: Nat. Provident Institution, British South Africa Co.

SIR GEO. SCHUSTER: Bank of N.Z., Eng., Scot. & Aust. Bank, Commercial Union Ass.

MARTINS

SIR HAROLD BIBBY (Ch.): Bibby Bros., Sea Ins.

E. R. BOWRING (DCh.): Royal, Liverpool, London & Globe Ins., Cunard.

SIR J. BROCKLEBANK (DCh.): Reliance Ins., Cunard (DCh.), Thos. Brocklebank.

D. I. CRAWFORD: Royal, Liverpool, London & Globe Ins., Wm. Crawford (Ch.).

EARL OF DERBY: London & Lancs. Ins., British Cotton Growing Ass. (Pres.).

SIR WM. GRAY: Liverpool, London & Globe, Wm. Gray (Ch.), South Durham Steel.

C. J. HOLLAND-MARTIN, M.P.: Lewis's Bank, Yorkshire Penny Bank, Standard Bank of S. Africa, Guardian Ass., Rhodesian Katanga (Ch.), Venesta.

J. A. HOLT: Sea Ins., Cunard (DCh.), Port Line.

T. H. NAYLOR: Royal, British & Foreign Marine Ins., West Indian Co., Demerara Co.

SIR JOHN N. NICHOLSON: Booker Bros., McConnell.

M. D. Oliphant: Sea Ins., Tate & Lyle.
M. Arnot Robinson: Reliance, Marine Ins., Coast Lines (Ch.).
P. D. Toosey: Cammell Laird, Combined English Mills.
Visct. Margesson (London Bd.): G.E.C., Assoc. Paper Mills, Tunnel Portland Cement.
Sir Nicholas Cayzer (London Bd.): Sea Ins., A.E.I., British & Commonwealth Shipping.
P. H. Muirhead (N.E. Board): Vickers.

BARCLAYS GROUP

A. W. Tuke (Ch.): Yorkshire Ins., Reinsurance Corp.
Sir F. C. Ellerton (DCh.): Yorkshire Penny Bank (DCh.).
C. Fitzherbert (VCh.): Barclays D.C.O., Atlas Ins.
Col. J. Thompson (VCh.): Alliance Ins., Agric. Mortgage Corp.
Earl of Airlie: British Linen Bank (Gov.), Life Ass. of Scotland, Jamaica Sugar Estates.
Earl Alexander: Phoenix Ass., Aluminium Co. of Canada.
T. D. Barclay: British Linen Bank, Alliance Ass.
A. C. Barnes: Barclays D.C.O. (DCh.), Eastern Bank, Phoenix Ass.
D. M. E. E. Bevan: Phoenix Ass., Evans & Bevan.
L. E. D. Bevan: Nat. Provident Institution, Barclay Perkins & Courage (Ch.), Styles & Winch (Ch.).
T. M. Bland: Clive Discount Bank (Ch.), Alliance Ass., Fisons, Tollemache (Ch.), E. Counties Building Society (DCh.).
Lord Cornwallis: Royal, Liverpool, London & Globe Ins., Warden Ins., A. E. Reed (Ch.), Fremlins.
J. S. Crossley: Barclays D.C.O. (Ch.), Imperial Bank of Canada, Mercantile & General Ins.
A. Denham: Halifax Building Society, Trafford Park Dwellings (Ch.).
Lord Dudley Gordon: Phoenix Ins., Hadfields, Millspaugh (Ch.), Manganese Steel, Commonwealth Development Corp.
Duke of Hamilton: British Linen Bank (DGov.), Norwich Union (Ch.).
Sir J. D. Horsfall: Lloyd's, Halifax Bldng. Society, Lanzil (Ch.).
Visct. Knollys: Employers Liability, Merchant Marine Ins., Clerical & Medical, General Reversionary Ins., Vickers (Ch.).
Sir Ernest Murrant: Economic Ins., Furness Withy (Ch.), Houlder Cairns Line (Ch.), Royal Mail (Ch.), Shaw Savill (DCh.), Pacific Steam (DCh.).
Visct. Portal: Barclays D.C.O., Commercial Union Ass., Ford Motors, British Aluminium (Ch.), N. British Aluminium (Ch.).
Frederick Seebohm: Barclays D.C.O. (VCh.), Century Ins., Gilletts Discount House.

EARL WOOLTON: Royal, Liverpool, London & Globe, Lewis's Investment Trust.

P. V. EMRYS EVANS (Barclays D.C.O. only): British S. Africa Co., Anglo-American Corp.

H. F. OPPENHEIMER (Barclays D.C.O. only): de Beers (Ch.), Anglo-American Corp., African Explosives, Rhokana, South African Mines Selection, Rand Selection, Broken Hill.

SIR THOS. ELLIS ROBINS (Barclays D.C.O. only): British South Africa Co. (Pres.), de Beers, Anglo-American Corp., Tanganyika Concessions, Wankie Colliery.

LORD CLYDESMUIR (British Linen Bank only): Scottish Provident Institution, Steel Co. of Scotland.

SIR JAMES MCNEILL (British Linen Bank only): National Shipbuilders Security, John Brown (Ch.).

SIR E. WEDDERBURN (British Linen Bank only): Scottish Prov. Institution, Shepperton & Wedderburn (Grants), Nether Pollock.

SIR GEO. WILSON (British Linen Bank only): Northern Ass., A. Bell.

WM. YOUNGER (British Linen Bank only): Wm. Younger, Wm. McEwan (Ch.).

R. M. LEE (Barclays Manchester Bd.): Calico Printers Ass. (Ch.), Lancs. Cotton Corp. (Ch.), Export Credits Advisory Council.

J. E. PEDDER (Barclays Local Bd.): Courtaulds.

C. H. G. MILLIS (Barclays Overseas Development Corp.): Sun, Sun Life Ass., Ind, Coope & Allsopp.

MIDLAND

VISCT. MONKTON (Ch.): Belfast Banking Co., Clydesdale & N. Scottish Bank.

LORD HARLECH: Bank of West Africa, Belfast Banking Co., Standard Bank of South Africa.

SIR ALEX. ROGER (DCh.): A. T. & T. (Ch.), British Insulated Callender's Cables (Pres.), Lisbon Electric Trams.

WM. DONALD (DCh.): U.K. Mutual Steamship Ins., Cunard (DCh.), Port Line (Ch.), Thos. Brocklebank.

S. J. ADAMS: Guardian Ass., Thos. Cook (Ch.), Bakelite (Ch.), Dean & Dawson (Ch.), HP, Lea & Perrins (Ch.).

VISCT. ALANBROOKE: National Discount Bank, Belfast Banking Co., Hudson's Bay.

SIR COLIN ANDERSON: Australia & N.Z. Bank, Marine Ins., Orient.

LORD BAILLEU: Eng., Scot. & Australian Bank, London & Lancs. Ins., Dunlop, Consolidated Zinc, General Mining & Investment.

LORD BLACKFORD: Guardian Ins., Ind, Coope & Allsopp, Grants.

SIR ALEX. FLECK: I.C.I. (Ch.), African Explosives (DCh.).

SIR JOHN HALL: Clerical, Medical & General Life Ins., P. & O., Meux Breweries, Trinidad & Limmer, Colonial Dev. Corp.

EARL OF FEVERSHAM: Clydesdale & N. Scottish Bank, Robt. Stephensons, Hutchinsons.

R. F. GLAZEBROOK: Royal, Liverpool, London & Globe.

SIR GEO. HARVIE WATT: Eagle Star Ins., Monotype (Ch.), Consolidated Goldfields (DCh.), Globe & Phoenix Gold Mining (Ch.), Australian Commonwealth Carbide.

SIR EDWARD HERBERT: Northern Ass., Wm. Hollins (DCh.), Viyella, N.C.B., E. Midlands Gas Bd.

J. P. HUNT: Eagle Star Ins., W. H. Smith (Engineers) (Ch.), John Hill (Ch.), Birmingham Chemicals (Ch.).

J. H. JOLLY: Powell Duffryn, Allied Ironfounders.

ROBT. LAIDLAW: Clydesdale & N. Scottish Bank (DCh.), J. & P. Coates (Ch.).

SIR FRANK MORGAN: Prudential (Ch.).

F. L. ORME: Royal, Liverpool, London & Globe, British & Foreign Marine Ins., Reynold & Gibson, British Cotton Growers Association.

H. L. ROUSE: Belfast Banking Co., London & Manchester Ass.

D. L. WHITNEY W. STRAIGHT: Rolls-Royce, Rotol.

D. W. TURNER: W. & T. Avery, Rollason Wire, Wellington Tube (Ch.), Victoria Tube (Ch.), Job Edwards (Ch.).

ADML. SIR PHILIP VIAN: North British Gp. Ins.

SIR HAROLD YARROW: Clydesdale & N. Scottish Bank, Yarrow & Co. (Ch.).

THREE BANKS GROUP

M. J. BARRINGTON-SMITH (DCh. Glyn Mills and R.B.S.): Bank of England, Ottoman Bank, Dalgety, A.E.I.

DUKE OF BUCCLEUCH, Gov. Royal Bank of Scotland.

ALEX. MAITLAND, Dep. Gov. Royal Bank of Scotland, Scottish Prov. Institution.

D. F. LANDALE (Ch. R.B.S., Glyn Mills, Wm. Deacon's):Northern Ass.

J. H. RICHARDSON(DCh. R.B.S.): Standard Life, U.S. Investment Corp.

EARL OF ELGIN (R.B.S. only): United Dominion Trust (Scots. Ch.), Scottish Ins.

SIR FRANCIS GLYN (Ch. Glyn Mills & R.B.S.): Bank of London & South America, Alliance Ass., Liebig, Oxo, Export Credit Advisory Council (DCh.).

L. A. ELGOOD (R.B.S. & Wm. Deacon's): Distillers, Alliance Box.

R. M. ROBERTSON (R.B.S. & Glyn Mills):Wm. Thyne, Electronic Trust.

K. G. HOLDEN (R.B.S. & Wm. Deacon's): British Empire Boiler & Electric Ins., Geigy Holdings.

T. G. WATERLOW (R.B.S. only): Standard Life, R. & R. Clark, Wm. Thyne.

SIR RONALD CAMPBELL (R.B.S. only): Anglo-Egyptian Oil.

SIR ERIC CARPENTER (R.B.S. & Wm. Deacon's Ch.): Yorkshire Penny Bank, London & Lancs. Ins., Grey Bros (Ch.).

D. H. CAMERON OF LOCHIEL (R.B.S. only): Scottish Widows Fund & Life, David MacBrayne, BTC.

J. M. PRAIN (R.B.S. only): Scottish Life Ins., James Prain (Ch.), Scottish Bd. for Industry, Scottish Gas Board.

EARL OF IVEAGH (R.B.S. Extraordinary Dir.): Arthur Guinness (Ch.).

SIR ERIC GORE BROWN (R.B.S. Extraordinary Dir. & Glyn Mills, Wm. Deacon's): Alexanders Discount Bank, Provincial & Mutual Life, Rio Tinto Mining.

SIR WM. C. CURRIE (R.B.S. Extraordinary Dir. & Wm. Deacon's): P. & O., Wm. Cory, Australian Steam Navigation, Suez Canal Co.

E. O. FAULKNER (Glyn Mills): Union Discount Bank, Richd. Thomas & Baldwins, Vickers, Hudson's Bay.

J. P. R. GLYN (Glyn Mills only): Agric. Mortgage Corp., Marine Ins., Exchange Telegraph, B.T.C. (Midlands).

J. N. HOGG (Glyn Mills only): Standard Bank of S. Africa, Gallaher, Borax.

C. G. RANDOLPH (Glyn Mills only): Sun (Ch.), Sun Life (Ch.), Planet, Elder Ins.

H. S. KERSHAW (Wm. Deacon's only): Joseph Holt & Yates Castle Breweries.

SIR KENNETH CROSSLEY (Wm. Deacon's only): Crossley (Ch.), A.C.V., Ocean Accident Ins.

SIR EDWIN S. HERBERT (Wm. Deacon's only): Yorkshire Ins. (DCh.), National Safe Deposit & Trustee Co. (Ch.), Broadcast Relay Services (Ch.), Associated Rediffusion, Enfield Cables, H. W. Herbert (Ch.), Ultramar, Walter Wanger.

SIR LESLIE ROBERTS (Wm. Deacon's only): Manchester Line, Vulcan Boiler & General Ins., Hick Hargreaves, Manchester Ship Canal (Ch.).

VISCT. SIMON (Wm. Deacon's only): P. & O. (DCh.), Australian, General Orient, Steam Navigation, Walker Sons, Port of London Authority.

P. L. WRIGHT (Wm. Deacon's only): Bleachers Association (Ch.), Commercial Plastics, Manchester Royal Exchange.

OTHER BANKERS

NATIONAL DISCOUNT

EARL OF LIMERICK: London Life Ass., Ascot Gas Co.

LORD McCORQUODALE: Bank of Scotland, McCorquodales, J. &. P. Coates, Spottiswoode & Ballantyne.

R. L. BASSETT: Siemens Ediswan, Alfred Graham.

UNION DISCOUNT

LORD KENNETT (Ch.): Equity & Law Life Ins., Law Reversionary Interest, Capital Issues Committee.

J. I. SPENS: Scottish Amicable Life Ins., John Summers, United Steel, London Tin Corp.

OTHERS (FROM 'TOP 50' COMPANIES ONLY)

SIR GEORGE BOLTON: Bank of England, Bank of London & S. America, Sun Life Ins., Consolidated Zinc.

GEOFFREY ELEY: Bank of England, British Bank of the M. E., Equity & Law Life Ins., Hawker Siddeley, Brush Group.

A. COMAR WILSON: Standard Bank of S. Africa, A.E.I., Anglo-American Corp., British S. African Co., S.W. Africa Co., Diamond Corp., Consolidated Mines.

LORD BILSLAND: Bank of Scotland (Gov.), Scottish Amicable Ass., John Brown, Colvilles, Burmah Oil.

SIR K. B. HARPER: Bank of Scotland, Shell, London Tin Corp.

I. M. STEWART, B.Sc.: National Bank of Scotland, Eagle Star, Babcock & Wilcox.

SIR BASIL GOULDING: National Bank, Hibernian Fire & Gen. Ins., Consolidated Zinc.

SIR D. BERNARD: British Bank of the M. E. (Ch.), Courtaulds.

SIR J. KEELING: London & Yorks Trust (Ch.), Bowaters, Cubitts (Ch.), B.E.A.

VISCT. DAVIDSON: Anglo-Portuguese Bank, Greshams Fire Ins., Dorman Long.

W. E. KEVILLE: National Bank of N.Z., Economic Ins., Furness Withy, Shaw Savill.

R. TILNEY: Ottoman Bank, Associated Portland Cement, H. W. Peabody (Ch.).

VISCOUNT BRUCE: National Bank of Australasia, Royal Exchange, P. & O.

COL. A. T. MAXWELL: Australia & N.Z. Bank (DCh.), Vickers, Steel Co. of Wales, English Steel Corp., Robt. Boby, Powers Samas, Cooke, Troughton & Simms.

W. C. WARWICK: Anglo-Portuguese Bank, Planet Ass. (Ch.), Furness Withy, Houlder Line (Ch.), Royal Mail (Ch.), Shaw Savill, Pacific Steam Navigation (Ch.).

SIR A. FORBES: Debenture Corp. (Ch.), Spillers, Shell, Iron & Steel Board (Ch.).

SIR EDWARD SPEARS: Bank of West Africa, Commercial Union Ass., Associated Portland Cement, British Bata Shoe (Pres.), Ashanti Goldfields (Ch.).

J. K. WEIR: Nat. Bank of Scotland, Dunlop.

NON-BANKING CONTROLLERS

IRON & STEEL

SIR JOHN GREEN: Thos. Firth & John Brown (Ch.), Richard Thomas & Baldwins, Staveley Coal & Iron, Wm. Beardmore (Ch.), E. Midlands Gas Board.

SIR GREVILLE MAGINNESS: Churchill Machine Tools (Ch.), Tube Investments (DCh.), Roneo (Ch.).

SIR ELLIS HUNTER: Royal Exchange Ass., Dorman Long (Ch.), Cleveland Trust (Ch.).

SIR HUGH BEAVER: Richard Thomas & Baldwins, Arthur Guinness, Colonial Development Corp.

A. REITH GRAY: John Summers (Gen. Mg.), Shelton Iron & Steel, Cammell Laird, Sea Insurance (Ch.).

H. H. MULLENS, B.Sc.: Dorman Long, Reyrolle (Mg.), Nuclear Power Plant (Jt. Mg.).

E. W. TOWLER: Cawoods (Ch.), Dorman Long, a dozen or more Quarry companies.

LORD REITH: Phoenix Ass., Tube Investments, British Oxygen, Colonial Development Corp. (Ch.).

SIR BRUCE GARDENER: Steel Co. of Wales (Md.), British Iron & Steel Corp. (Ch.), Consett Iron, Guest, Keen & Nettlefold, Crompton Parkinson (VCh.).

C. R. WHEELER: Guest, Keen & Nettlefold, John Lysaght, British Iron & Steel Corp., Ore Carriers, Wimpey, Tarmac, United Reinsurers.

N. H. ROLLASON: John Summers (Mg.), United Steel, Iron & Steel Board.

LORD DYNEVOR: Sun Ins., Richard Thomas & Baldwins.
R. T. PEMBERTON: Richard Thomas & Baldwins, Pressed Steel.
SIR R. BARLOW: Metal Box (Ch.), Steel Co. of Wales.

SHIPPING

R. A. VESTEY: Union International (Ch.), Albion Ins. (Ch.), Booth
Steamships (Ch.), Blue Star Line (Ch.).
F. L. CHARLTON: Cunard, Furness Withy (DCh.), Royal Mail, Shaw
Savill, Pacific Steam Navigation (DCh.), Whitehall Ins.
LORD GEDDES: P. & O., Limmer & Trinidad, Scottish Union and
American Union Ass., Scottish Gas Board.

DISTILLING & BREWING

SIR G. HAYMAN: Distillers Co. (Ch. Bd. Management), United
Molasses, BX Plastics, British Plaster Bd., Tankers, Ltd.
G. W. SCOTT: Distillers Co., United Molasses (Ch.), Anchor Line,
Tankers, Ltd. (Ch.), W. Indies Sugar Co.
LORD TEDDER: Distillers Co., Standard Motor Co. (Ch.).
HON. P. REMNANT: Ind, Coope & Allsopp (Ch.), Assam Co. (Ch.),
Dalgety.
E. THOMPSON: Ind, Coope & Allsopp (Ch.), Sun, Sun Life Ass.
H. L. BRADFER LAWRENCE: Ind, Coope & Allsopp, Guardian Ass.

TEXTILES, ETC.

SIR JOHN HANBURY WILLIAMS: Bank of England, Courtaulds (Ch.),
Snia Viscosa.
C. F. KEARTON: Courtaulds, British Celanese, U.K. Atomic Energy
Authority.
J. S. BULLIMORE: Patons & Baldwins (Ch.), J. & P. Coates.
F. LE NEVE FOSTER: Van Heusen (Ch.), Stewarts & Lloyds.
G. E. BEHARRELL: Dunlop (Ch.), Goodyear (Ch.), India (Ch.), Iron
& Steel Board.

FOOD, TOBACCO, DISTRIBUTION

SIR LAWRENCE CADBURY: Bank of England, British Cocoa & Chocolate,
Daily News.
CHARLES CLORE: Sears Holdings (Ch.), Freeman, Hardy & Willis
(Ch.), etc., etc.
ISAAC WOLFSON: G.U.S. (Ch.), etc., etc., etc.
L. A. RENFELL: G.U.S., etc., etc.
C. A. GARBUTT: G.U.S., etc., etc.
JOHN BEDFORD: Debenhams (Ch.), etc., Zürich Ins.

J. O. COLLINS: Debenhams, etc., etc.

VISCT. TENBY: Ranks the Millers, Associated Portland Cement.

LORD SINCLAIR: Imperial Tobacco (Ch.), British American Tobacco, Finance Corp. for Industry, Commonwealth Development Finance.

LORD COLERAINE: Boots the Chemists, Northern Ins., Atomic Power Construction (Ch.), United Premier Oil & Cake, Ascot Heaters, Horlicks.

RT. HON. GEOFFREY SHAKESPEARE: Associated Portland Cement, London Brick, Abbey National Blding. Soc.

ELECTRICAL ENGINEERING

LORD CHANDOS: Alliance Ins., A.E.I. (Ch.), I.C.I.

LORD WEEKS: Royal Exchange, Finance Corp. for Industry, A.E.I., Vickers, Pilkingtons, Massey Harris, B.P. (Govt. Director).

S. F. BURMAN: Burman's Production Engineers, Joseph Lucas, W. & T. Avery, I.C.I., Midlands Electricity Bd.

LESLIE C. GAMAGE: G.E.C. (Ch.), Pirelli (Ch.), Siemens.

SIR E. WILSHAW: English Electric, Victory Ins., West, East & South African Telegraph Cos. (Ch.), Cable & Wireless.

SIR E. SPEED: A.E.I., British Celanese, Dalgety.

J. SPENCER WILLS: British Electric Traction (DCh.), Monotype (DCh.), Broadcast Relay Services, Assoc. Rediffusion (Ch.).

R. P. BEDDOW: British Electric Traction, Broadcast Relay, Assoc. Rediffusion.

W. T. JAMES: British Electric Traction, Broadcast Relay, Assoc. Rediffusion.

BRIG. THE RT. HON. ANTHONY HEAD: A.E.I.

D. W. ALDRIDGE: British Insulated Callender's Cables, Philips Electrical Industries.

SIR ED. CROWE: English Electric, Saml. Courtauld.

SIR A. BOYD: A.E.I., Cammell Laird.

NON-ELECTRICAL ENGINEERING

SIR H. WILSON SMITH: Guest, Keen & Nettlefold, Powell Duffryn, Wm. Cory, N.C.B.

SIR J. R. YOUNG: Vickers, B.S.A., Borg Warner, James Booth (VCh.), Metropolitan Cammell, Pinchin & Johnson, S. Smiths, G. Mann.

A. H. HIRD, B.Sc.: Vickers, Metropolitan Cammell, Cooke, Troughton & Simms, R. Boby, J. Olding, A.B.C. Motors.

SIR T. OVERY: Powell Duffryn, Handley Page, Technicolor, Ten Test.

LORD AIREDALE: Ford Motors, John Dickinson, London Ass.

LORD BRIDGES: Babcock & Wilcox, Equity & Law Life Ins.

BASIL SANDERSON: Bank of England, Ford Motors, Furness Withy, Shaw Savill, Economic Planning Board.

SIR HARRY PILKINGTON: Bank of England, Pilkingtons (Ch.), Triplex, etc.

J. C. GRIDLEY: Powell Duffryn, Mobiloil (Ch.).

SIR F. PICKWITH: Vickers, English Steel Corp. (Ch.).

E. J. WADDINGTON: Vickers, English Steel Corp.

OVERSEAS COMPANIES

R. B. HAGERT: London & Lancs. Ins., de Beers, Anglo-American Corp., Rand Selection, Rhodesian Anglo-American.

LORD TWEEDSMUIR: Nat. Provident Institution, Dalgety, Bovril, B.O.A.C.

E. F. M. BUTLER: London & Lancs. Ins., Anglo-American Debenture Corp., Corp. of Foreign Bondholders (Dir. Gen.), Antofagasta Rlwy.

MARQUESS OF WILLINGDON: Albion Ins., Humber, Antofagasta Rlwy.

Sources: Stock Exchange Year Book 1958; Directory of Directors 1958.

Notes: (1) Only major companies listed. (2) Directors of Banks who do not sit on major companies' boards excluded.

(Reproduced by kind permission from *The University and Left Review*.)

Parliament and the Establishment

by Christopher Hollis

Age 56. Assistant Editor of *Punch*. For ten years Conservative M.P. for Devizes. Author of *Along the Road to Frome* (autobiography), *Can Parliament Survive?*, and many other political works and biographies. Roman Catholic. Married, three sons, one daughter.

THE word 'establishment' is a word more frequently used these days than it is accurately defined. I have not yet read the other essays in this volume, and whether their writers are defining Establishment in exactly the same sense as I, I cannot say. All that I can do is to give my own definition and so make it clear about what I am writing.

By Establishment I mean then a body of people, acting, consciously or subconsciously, together, holding no official posts through which they exercise their power but nevertheless exercising a great influence on national policy. It is our concern to decide whether there is such an influence acting, so far as this essay goes, on our Parliamentary life—if there be such an influence, whether it is good or bad—and, if bad, how it can be counteracted. We have no right to beg the question by assuming that all ambient influences are evil influences. Some are good and necessary. Each must be considered on its own merits.

Now it is of course a commonplace that our government is party government and that nevertheless the party system is unknown to the formal constitution. The voter goes to the poll and is confronted with the names of William Jones and Thomas Smith on the voting paper. There is no description of them there and he has theoretically to make his choice between two individuals. Yet everyone knows that Mr. Jones is the Conservative candidate and Mr. Smith is the Labour candidate, and the great majority of the voters do not pretend that they are in reality voting for an individual. They are, as they confess, either voting Labour or voting Conservative. The successful candidate comes up to Westminster. Again the theory of the constitution knows nothing of him save that he is a Member of Parliament. Hansard reports his speeches, recording his constituency but making no mention of his party. When a division is called, he can in theory choose for himself the lobby which he will patronize. But again everybody knows that he takes his seat among the members of his own party and that he regularly receives instructions from his Whip how he shall vote and in the overwhelming majority of cases obeys those instructions. We need not waste our time on these formalities which are familiar.

The question is 'Who are really the masters now?' and that is a question which it is by no means simple to answer. The elector goes to the poll and, as I say, makes his choice between Mr. Jones, the Conservative candidate, and Mr. Smith, the Labour candidate, but why Mr. Jones is the Conservative and Mr. Smith is the Labour candidate he has as a general rule not the faintest idea. All he knows is that he opened the paper one day and read that these two gentlemen had been selected. Selected by whom or how? The great majority of voters would have but a very shadowy notion. They have of course been selected by the executive of the Conservative Association and by the General Management Committee of the local Labour Party. These consist of a small knot of party enthusiasts—for all practical purposes self-nominated. They select the candidate—which means that in a safe seat they virtually nominate the Member of Parliament. Every now and again, as with the Conservatives in East Bournemouth or with the Labour Party recently at St. Helens, there is a public outcry at the choice that they have made; there are demands for a primary election, for a more democratic method of selection, complaints that meetings have been packed and the rest. But in the vast majority of cases the selected candidate is merely accepted without question. If the members of the executive can virtually nominate themselves to office, it is not that they hold power by bribery or intimidation. It is simply that party politics in between elections are so boring that only a handful of enthusiasts is willing to take an interest in them and to go to meetings. Those who go to meetings get given the party posts. The rest of the voters—the 99 per cent of mugwumps—may be more balanced in opinion than the political enthusiasts, but they can hardly complain that it is the enthusiasts who nominate the candidates. Now it is obvious that the enthusiasts are likely to be extreme supporters of their party's policy, and so as a general rule an extremist in either direction—a Conservative of the extreme Right or a Socialist of the extreme Left—has a better chance of selection than a moderate. Major Frend was for a time preferred to Mr. Nicolson in Bournemouth and Mr. Zilliacus is preferred to Sir Frank

Soskice in Gorton, and, even though the central party machines should wish it otherwise, there is little that they can do about it. Their powers over the selection of candidates are small and negative. They can refuse to endorse a candidate whose opinions are too wildly unorthodox. But they cannot impose a candidate on a constituency whose local executive is unwilling to accept him. There have been several examples in recent months of leaders of parties and Central Offices failing to obtain the adoption of candidates whom they favoured. Mr. Gaitskell would like to have such supporters as Mr. Woodrow Wyatt and Mr. Crosland in the House but for a long time he could not get constituencies to adopt them.

At first sight then it might appear that those who take the trouble to serve on local executives are important and powerful people, but of course it is not so, and no one who has ever been to a meeting of a local party executive could be under any illusion that he is seeing a meeting of the Establishment. Wherever the Establishment is, it is not there. The reason why they are not important is that, though they have great power in deciding who becomes a Member of Parliament, the Member of Parliament when he is elected, is himself without influence.

The catalogue of arguments for and against party discipline at Westminster is tolerably familiar. It is of course true that the Member receives from the Whips instructions how to vote (except for the very rare occasions when there is a free vote) and that it requires obstinacy and courage to defy those instructions even to the extent of abstaining—often almost heroism to defy them to the extent of voting against your party. It is true that so large a part of the time of all debates is taken up by Front Bench speeches that the chances of a back bencher getting called in a major debate are so small that most Members give up the attempt to intervene in frustrated despair. It is true, to set against that, that back benchers have certain limited opportunities to raise subjects of their choice, when the ballot favours them, on private members' motions, or on adjournment debates, but such opportunities only come to the lucky few and, even when they come, the back bench Member may derive what satisfaction he can from seeing his speech reported in Hansard or in the local Press but he knows very well that he has almost no chance of getting any legislation on the Statute Book unless the Government co-operates with him in giving him facilities. He can put down questions at question time—and this is on the whole his most useful privilege—but even then the Minister can always check his curiosity by saying 'That does not arise out of the question on the Order paper' or 'I must have notice of that question' and passing on to the next. The Member who persists in his supplementaries is not only unpopular with the Speaker and with the Ministers, but he is also unpopular with other private Members who fear that, if he takes up too much time, their questions will not be reached. Thus the procedure skilfully sets private Member against private Member.

There are of course those who say that, though the back bench Member has no influence on the floor of the House, he can greatly influence his party's policy by his speeches upstairs in private committees. There is some truth in this. It is a very disgraceful truth. The machinery of a democratic government is supposed to be a public machinery. Our representatives are supposed to give their votes in public, where all the world can see. It is a disgraceful thing that Members of Parliament should express and vote for their real opinions in private behind closed doors and then come and give a merely automatic support to the party line in public. Yet it does to some extent happen, and there have been examples since the war—C licences under the Socialists, the Shops Bill or Teachers' Superannuation under the Conservatives—where back bench pressure has compelled a Government to change its policy. There has only been one example—capital punishment—where action by back benchers on the floor of the House has affected Government policy. There, though the abolitionists were not able to get on to the Statute Book the full measure which they favoured, at any rate they were able to compel the Government to do more than it wished to do.

Yet in general no one could seriously deny that the power of the executive over Parliament is so large as to be almost absolute, and that a back bench Member of Parliament has not sufficient to do to make it, if he has a serious interest in politics, worth his while to stay there very long. Either he uses the back benches as a stepping stone to office, or, if he does not wish for or is unable to attain office, like, for instance, Sir Hartley Shawcross, he drops out. A few still stay on, using the House more or less as their club, but it is no longer a very good club.

Why, it is asked, are the back benchers so docile? By what

sanctions are the Whips able to enforce their discipline? There is of course no single answer. As in all human actions, the motives range from the honourable to the discreditable. It is hard to say in judgement on another in what proportion these motives have been intermixed in any particular case. It is even harder for a man to assess the proportions of his own motives. Loyalty is in itself a virtue, but for that very reason it is fatally easy to make it the excuse for cowardice or the toleration of injustice.

Obviously the Whips have no power of physical compulsion. If any attempt was made physically to prevent a Member from going into the lobby in opposition to his party or from walking out of the House, it would be a gross breach of privilege. It is indeed far from certain whether, if a Member chose to raise the matter, he could not make a good case in law that the methods of moral persuasion now employed are in breach of privilege, but nobody does raise it. But what can a Whip or the party leaders do to a Member who defies them? They can in the last resort with-draw the Whip from him—that is to say, cease to recognize him as a member of the party. This is in fact hardly ever done in the Conservative Party and, although from time to time the Whip is withdrawn in the Labour Party, it is almost always restored again before the general election. The threat contained in a withdrawal of the Whip is of course that the member, no longer being in good standing with the party, will not be adopted in his constituency at the next election. But it is a dangerous card for the Whips and the Central Offices to play, for it all depends on circumstances how it will work out. It may be—particularly if like the Suez rebels among the Conservatives or the Bevanites of the old days among the Socialists, the rebellious member stands for a stronger policy than that of the party—that his constituents will prefer him to the party line. Then Central Office will look foolish. Or again, if it conducts a bitter personal campaign against the member in his constituency, then he can always spite it by standing as an Independent against the regular party candidate and possibly presenting the seat to the other party. So, taking it all in all, the withdrawal of the Whip is not a very effective weapon and indeed I can hardly recall any politician who has been driven out of Parliamentary life by such a withdrawal. Where a Whip is with-drawn it is usually withdrawn at the request of a discontented member himself and then, as with both the Bevanites and the

Suez group, these essays at independence on both sides are usually short-lived and the revolting members are back in their respective parties long before an election comes along.

A much more effective discipline is exercised by the fact that in the Whips' hands lies the disposal of every amenity which makes life at Westminster tolerable. It is not necessary for the Whip to be so crude as to say: 'If you oppose the party policy, you need not hope for that under-secretaryship, bang go your chances of a knighthood, you cannot expect to be included on any of our delegations abroad or to serve on the committee on that subject in which you are especially interested.' But everyone knows that that threat is there and it is effective. Life at Westminster, if it is not alleviated by some special assignments from time to time, is unendurably boring, and the Whips, who make these assignments, thus always have it in their power to kill the rebel by a positive Chinese torture of boredom.

There are other pressures. So long as every vote is treated as a vote of confidence, then an adverse vote, on whatever subject, means the resignation of the Government. 'Do you want to turn the Government out and put those fellows in?' The days of the philosophic M.P. are gone. The great majority of Members do not follow public affairs in great detail and have not got opinions of their own on most of the subjects discussed. They are executives and administrators rather than philosophers, interested in doing rather than in thinking. Their attitude towards Parliament is much more the attitude of a player of a game than of a statesman. In the House one has to sit in proximity to the members of one's own party. Nothing is more unpleasant than to sit side by side day after day with people who think that you are behaving like a traitor. It is probably this motive more than any other which both leads Members to be reluctant to oppose their party except when the gravest issues compel them and also in many cases to be anxious to leave Parliament rather to continue in an atmosphere that is so unnecessarily unpleasant.

Anyway, whatever the reason, the fact is certainly that a back bench Member of Parliament can perhaps sometimes find some minor non-party issue, such as Dr. Johnson has found in mental health, on which he can concentrate his useful attention, but on all major issues there is a party line which sometimes varies bewilderingly from day to day and there seems quite literally no limit to the subservience with which the vast majority of members of a party is willing to accept instructions on how it should vote. The *reductio ad absurdum* of party discipline was seen in the Conservative party's behaviour over Suez. The Suez adventure may have been right or it may have been wrong, but the vast majority of Conservatives was willing to vote for going into Suez one day and for coming out a few days afterwards, for asserting that we should never allow the Canal to be under the sole control of Nasser and for allowing it to remain under the sole control of Nasser. Mr. Butler commends the Conservative Government to the public with the words: 'Never has there been a time in the world's history when clear, determined leadership was more important, and that is what we propose to give you.' Mr. Butler is the Betjeman of politics. Neither he nor anybody else can ever be quite certain when he is being funny and when he is being serious.

It was not of course that all Conservative Members—perhaps that any Conservative Members in or out of the Government— agreed with every one of the steps that were taken at Suez. Notoriously they did not and in their private conversations they were outspoken in their criticisms. I remember a conversation with a Member who said that he did not see how 'any sane person' could support the Suez policy. Yet, as he confessed, he had obediently voted for every one of its successive stages and uttered no word of criticism in the House, in his constituency or elsewhere. His argument was the argument to which I referred, that the only consequence of a rebellious vote could have been to put 'the other fellows'—the Socialists—in, but, if no vote is ever to be cast on the merits of the question upon which the vote is taken, Parliamentarians cannot expect the public to take their system very seriously.

So there is, I think, little dispute about it that party discipline is now so strong at Westminster that the ordinary politician cannot reasonably be called a free man. When we look at the experience of other countries that have abolished Parliaments, we cannot wish to follow in their footsteps. It is certainly a much lesser evil to have Parliament than not to have it. Yet we are living in a fool's paradise if we think that it can possibly go on as it is at present, if no remedy is found for its absurdities. The question is, Is the situation irremediable? Of course it is not. True there has never been a Parliamentary system in any country where there have not

G

been some sort of party organizations, but that does not mean that the party system, as we know it in this country at this time, is a necessity of nature. In other countries parties are formed and reformed to fight the particular issues of the moment. Only in Britain and America has the monstrous notion of a party with a continuing life ever been envisaged. In Britain and America the parties are not formed to carry through a policy. The parties exist in their own right and then search about, as elections come along, to discover what policies to champion. That is an absurdity that is bound to lead to a sterility of political life. Nor is it in the least true that voting has always been as strictly disciplined as it is today. Without going back to the far freer days of the nineteenth century, it is only necessary to look at the statistics collected by Dr. Johnson in the appendix to the *Doctor in Parliament* to see how much counter-voting there was in the pre-1914 Parliament. Indeed there was even a good deal of counter-voting in the 1945 Parliament. It is only since 1950 that the discipline of the vote has been tightened up to the extreme of absurdity. Nor is it of course in the least true that the two-party system is in some way natural to this country any more than it is to other countries. The Labour party and the Irish Nationalists were only the largest minority groups before 1914; until then there had always been a substantial number of Members who did not accept the discipline of either of the main parties, and it was the presence of these dissidents which was largely responsible for the preservation of reality in debate. In fact it is only since 1945 that we have had anything like a two-party system in this country in the sense that the overwhelming majority of members belonged to one or other of the two main parties—and only since 1945 that Parliament has been in headlong decline.

Similarly, if the masters of the two parties wish electors to have a more real say in who shall be the Members who represent them, all that they have to do is to introduce the alternative vote. With the alternative vote, not only would candidates who do not belong to one or other of the two main parties have a better chance of election but also there would be no reason why more than one candidate of the Conservative or of the Socialist party should not present himself. The Conservative or the Socialist voters could then with their first preference make the choice of the candidate of their own party which they prefer without running any risk that by doing so they will present the seat to the opposite party. There is no difficulty whatsoever about introducing this reform. It is simply that the masters of the machines do not want to introduce it.

There are not then many who would question the proposition that life at Westminster is almost entirely controlled by party discipline. A much more interesting question—a question to which the answer is far less certain—is the question, What is the party system? Do we find at Westminster two armies, devotees of totally opposite philosophies, arrayed against one another, determined to fight out to the death their battle for the future of the country and therefore reasonably imposing on their members discipline in the detail of the carrying out of the grand strategic plan on which all are agreed? Or is the truth rather more like that suggested by Hilaire Belloc and Cecil Chesterton before the 1914 war? Is the fight rather a sham fight? Are the two front benches playing a game and intent rather on keeping the game going, in taking it turn and turn about to be in office rather than they are in imposing any particular policy on the state? And, if so, who is really the master of the state? Who are the gods behind the gods to whose tune the politicians, nominally in office and nominally in opposition, obediently dance? Is there in short an Establishment?

There are of course times when the changing face of things demands the reshaping of society. The years between 1945 and 1950 were such a time. Then there are real battles in Parliament and clear-cut issues which perhaps make it reasonable that Parliament should at any rate be dominated by two main parties. It is at such times reasonable to say that a man must be on one side or the other. But there are also far longer periods of doldrums, in which there are no clear-cut issues and in which the party divisions no longer correspond to reality. The years since 1950 have been such a period. There is no great difference in policy between the parties. There is not even, as Mr. Mackenzie has shown, any great difference in organization. The only difference is a difference of manner. The Labour party thinks of itself as a party of a creed and therefore, even when it has not got a creed, it likes to behave as if it had one. Its tradition is therefore a tradition of very great personal disloyalty to its leader, combined with great expressions of loyalty to the mystic party. The Conservative party on the other hand thinks of itself rather as a regiment than as a Church. The typical Conservative is therefore ready to follow his leader into or out of any conceivable position and it is to him rather a matter of pride, than the reverse, if today's position is the exact opposite of that of yesterday. It proves, he thinks, that the policy is 'flexible' and not 'doctrinaire', and anyway not his to reason why. It is enough for him to follow the colonel.

That there are forces behind both political parties that exercise a very powerful influence upon their policies is not of course disputable. The Socialists, as Mr. Crossman found to his cost, dare not offend, and dare not tell the truth about, the trades unions, for it is the trades unions who supply the money for their activities. The Conservatives are equally unable to offend the moneyed interests on which they rely. Then behind both parties are the civil servants. In theory the political Minister is master and the civil servants are merely his servants, carrying out his orders. In practice every Government department is stocked with senior officials who say, 'Of course, if you say so, Minister, but, if you insist, of course you understand that it will upset the whole traditional method of running this department and that the inconveniences will be insuperable' for this reason and that reason. The civil servant has been in the Ministry for a generation; the Minister came in last week. The affairs of ministries are today intolerably complicated. It is only a very self-confident Minister who will more than once or twice be brave enough to stand up against his civil servants. Thus Home Secretary after Home Secretary supported the abolition of capital punishment before he was in office and supports it again when he is out of office. But the Home Office is notoriously opposed to the reform and Home Secretaries are not found strong enough to support the reform when they are in office.

Yet the power of bureaucracy, real as it is, is not what we generally mean by the Establishment. The essence of the Establishment, as the phrase has come to be used, is that it consists of people who exercise power without having any official position which entitles them to do so. Is there such an Establishment operating in our Parliamentary life? By making the answer melodramatic one can easily make it ridiculous. If it be meant, do secret meetings from time to time take place at which the Prime Minister, the Leader of the Opposition, the Chief Whips and the Speaker consult with, say, the Archbishop of Canterbury, the Warden of All Souls, the President of the M.C.C. and the Editor of *The Times* to decide exactly who shall say what in Parliament and how the votes shall go, of course no such meetings do take place; and indeed I am not at all sure that the word 'establishment' is not a confusing word to introduce into this inquiry. It implies that there is a definite small, private body which exercises power and that, if only we knew enough facts, we could all know who were its exercisers. But much more in England is done by subconscious influence than by conscious decision, much more by ambient feeling than by identifiable conspirators, such as the word 'establishment' suggests. The power of the Establishment, such as it is, comes not from the fact that a dozen people impose their will on the rest of us but from the fact that there is in all of us a degree of establishment-mindedness—that we feel it right that the opinions of such persons should have attention paid to them.

It would obviously be an absurd naivete to imagine that the conventional story of the bitter battle between the two parties, each only anxious to defeat the other, is the whole truth. It would be as false to imagine that the whole story is a total and conscious fraud. The truth is that every Parliamentarian must necessarily have a double loyalty. He has a loyalty to his party and he has also a loyalty to the system, and this double loyalty imposes on him an inevitable dilemma. As a party man, he must say and, what makes it much more difficult, believe—for it is beyond the capacity of human nature to live one's whole life with the tongue in the cheek—that the most important thing in the world is that his party should get into power, the greatest of calamities that the other party should get into power. As a believer in the Parliamentary system, he must know very well that the condition of its health and continuance is that the parties should take it turn and turn about to be in power. Like an experienced and philosophical schoolmaster, he can indeed both believe in general that it is a healthy thing that his and a rival school should share their rugger victories out fairly equally over the years and at the same time be passionately anxious that his school should gain the victory on any particular afternoon. But it is difficult—though not impossible—for grown men to be immature all the time. Again, at any rate in present conditions, the politician must know that the international and the economic situations are both so delicate that no British Government has much room for manœuvre. Whatever may have been true in other and more carefree days, when no one could get to England except in a ship and we had many more ships than anyone else, when we had ample foreign investments to cushion us against temporary difficulties in the balance of trade, today we are only to a very limited extent masters in our own house. Therefore any British Government, Conservative or Socialist, has over the greater part of the field to pursue very much the same policy as its rival. It is not possible to pursue a policy which unduly divides the nation. On the other hand the people who take an active part in politics in the constituencies—the members of the Conservative and the Socialist executives—are people who from their opposite sides are calling on their leaders to pursue just those extreme policies which the leaders know very well would destroy the country, and for political reasons these people have up to a point from time to time to be placated by flattering speeches. Therefore the first task of any Prime Minister of this country today, Conservative or Socialist, is to pursue a policy often the opposite of that which is demanded by his supporters and to prevent his supporters from noticing it. How brilliantly has this task been performed by Mr. Macmillan! How adroitly is Mr. Gaitskell preparing to perform it in his turn, with the careful hint, dropped nobody quite knows by whom, that after the next election the Socialists may find themselves faced with a prospect of 'office without power!'.

It is one example of that growing gap between the language which those who govern the nation use when they are talking among themselves in private and the language which they use in public which Mr. Crossman has rightly noted as an especial mark of our age. 'It is democracy, ironically enough', he writes, 'which has created the gaping abyss that now divides the published political myth from the unpublishable political reality. As early as 1870 Bagehot pointed to the contrast between the semblance and the reality of power in British politics. Since his epoch Parliamentary Government has been replaced by what can be described as alternating party dictatorship, if one uses "dictatorship" not in the pejorative but in the Roman sense of the word. Our modern system of highly centralized Cabinet Government is now buttressed by a party system which limits the elector to choosing between the Cabinet and the Shadow Cabinet; which has steadily degraded the status of the individual M.P. and which, most serious of all, is rapidly transferring both debate and decision from the publicity of the floor of the Commons to the secrecy of the party caucus in the committee room upstairs or the party headquarters outside.'

Now this Butskellite policy, as it used to be called, is not necessarily dishonourable—is not indeed even necessarily wrong. I myself would argue that, by and large, it is right, but it can only be pursued by a statesman who is prepared and able to indulge in very devious twists and turns. We have Abraham Lincoln's word for it that 'you cannot fool all of the people all of the time', but one is bound to admit that our post-war politicians make a very good attempt at performing this feat. It is with its effect on the Parliamentary debate that we are here concerned. That the debate is of no immediate moment, since whatever is said, the division that follows it will run along preordained and party lines, is of course well understood, but I am concerned with a somewhat deeper point—with the futility of the modern party debate in itself. The pretence is that the Government proposes its measure and that the Opposition marshals any argument of which it can think to expose the futility of that measure and that thus truth is exposed by the exposure of the strongest arguments on either side. The reality bears little relation to that. The reality is that on almost all the great issues of the day opinion within each party is divided. Therefore neither party is anxious to discuss the issue at all if it can help it for fear that a discussion would reveal its own divisions. What is odder still is that neither party is really very anxious to expose with any vigour the divisions of its opponent, because, if it did so, the opponent would retaliate and expose its divisions. The overwhelming object of the masters of both parties is to avoid an open split. This is more important than immediate victory, for the Opposition and the Government both know that, if only the Opposition remains apparently united and if only the game is kept going, it is bound to have its turn sooner or later. It is to the interest of the leaders of both parties to keep the game going with the teams substantially as they are now. If there were an open split, then there would be a redeal of the parties, and who can say whether the present leaders would be still leaders in the new set-up? So, when the great crises of the day are debated, the debate does not rage around the important questions that are in everybody's mind. Those questions remain strangely unasked. Thus for instance take the great issue whether this country should have the H-bomb. There are strong arguments for and strong arguments against. The issue is as important as any with which we have ever been faced. We must choose one way or the other and our whole survival—indeed the whole survival of the human race—may well depend on our choosing rightly. The simpleton would have imagined that, if ever there was an issue on which the Opposition would demand from a Government the frankest debate it was to be found here. Yet what happens? What happens is that the Socialists, far from demanding such a debate, take every opportunity that they can to avoid it. If the matter has to be debated at all, instead of either frankly opposing or frankly supporting the Government, they prefer to concentrate on the entirely secondary demand that there should be a delay in the testing of the H-bombs that have already been made—an issue that cannot conceivably have more than a limited bearing on the situation and which is obviously chosen not because it is important but because it is unimportant. The reason, as we all understand, is that opinion on the possession of the H-bomb is very evenly divided within the Socialist party. Therefore the Socialists have no wish that those divisions should be advertised, as they would be if the subject were debated. Or turn to the Conservatives. All the most important members of the present Government were members of the Government at the time of Suez. They did not resign. From time to time they have made statements to say that the action taken at Suez was justified and that, if it failed of complete success, it only failed because of the unpatriotic opposition of the Socialists. Yet on the most charitable of interpretations there is much in the Government's policy at Suez which is far from clear. If the full story is a story which would show that the Government was abundantly justified, one would have thought that here, if ever, the usual precedent would have been followed. A White Paper, setting out all the facts—facts which on this hypothesis would have justified the Government in all that they did—would have been issued and the Socialists would have been dared to challenge this uncontrovertible case on the floor of the House. Nothing of the sort has been done. Why not? No one doubts that the reason is that, though all who were in the Government at the time of Suez and are in the Government still, have to take formal responsibility for all that was done, in fact there are members of the Government who think that indefensible blunders were committed and who therefore prefer that as little should be said about it as possible.

Now this attitude, though not perhaps very glorious, is at least intelligible. But what is wholly extraordinary is not so much that the Government should be reluctant to publish its defence of its conduct as that the Opposition should be almost as reluctant to demand that they should do so—that, though in general terms the Socialists at the time denounced the action at Suez as wholly disreputable, it should yet, when that action is proved a failure, allow its whole case to go by default and leave it to Mr. Randolph Churchill in a newspaper to expose the failure with no serious support except from a few highly irregular Socialist back benchers.

One could pile up further instances almost *ad nauseam*. There is for instance the reluctance of both front benches to have a discussion about the Common Market and the Free Trade area. Both parties have promised that the Coal Board must be made to pay its way and both front benches know very well that they have no hope of making it do so. Therefore they prefer to talk about coal as little as possible, and in default of such issues, at a time when the very foundations of civilization are in jeopardy, the House prefers to spend days on end talking about the use of motor cars at elections and who tore O.H.M.S. off the top of an envelope.

As a result Parliament has almost ceased to function as a real element in our political life. Those who have real issues to raise, raise them on the radio or in the Press but no longer on the floor of the House. A serious, if cynical, case can be made out for it that this extinction of Parliament is under modern conditions inevitable. It may be argued that our condition is so critical and our problems so complex that it is essential to leave all reality of power in the hands of an untrammelled executive, that no better way of doing this can be found than by allowing nominal power to be held, turn and turn about, by two parties who pursue essentially the same policy, that an impotent Parliament which has a nominal but no real control over the executive gives to the people an illusion of self-government which has a psychological convenience but carries with it no threat of real interference—that the executive is indeed much more secure against interference with its omnipotence under such a two-party system with a bogus legislature than it would be under a one-party system with a public opinion that noticed the threat to its liberties in the overt abolition of the traditional legislature. This I believe to be very largely true, and indeed it must in fairness be confessed that, if the politicians habitually evade the discussion of the really important issues on the floor of the House, it is not merely through fear of the exposure of the skeletons in their cupboards that they do so. Day after day, whether the debate be on international affairs or on industrial affairs at home, we hear Ministers in the House get up and say, "I must ask the Right Honourable gentleman not to press me on that point. Very important discussions are at this moment taking place and it would not be in the public interest to make a statement at this moment". The request is almost always granted. What alternative has the questioner but to grant it? And of course the Minister on most particular occasions is perfectly justified in making the request. We have moved into a state of affairs where decisions on almost every topic of importance are taken not by a decision of the House of Commons but as a result of negotiations with various relevant and powerful outside bodies. It is hard to see how that situation could possible be reversed to any important extent, and for each particular by-passing of Parliament there is always a serious and solid case to be made. But the total result of all these acts of by-pass is that Parliament has been rendered almost entirely impotent. Is that inevitable? Is it desirable?

Fully admitting all the obvious inconveniences of freedom, I nevertheless do not think that it is either inevitable or desirable. The condition of Parliamentary impotence is the two-party system. As long as virtually all the Members of Parliament belong to one or other of the two main parties that are going to take it turn and turn about to be in office, the unreality of the Parliamentary debate is almost inevitable. But, if there is, as there has been throughout all history up till 1945, a sizeable body of Members who belong to some other party or parties, those Members can render an incalculable service to Parliament by insisting on dragging out of the cupboards these skeletons which both parties wish to keep hidden there, by forcing reality to break in on Parliament's debates. It is not necessary that these independent Members should hold a voting balance between the two parties. It is probably better that they should not hold such a balance. The essential service that they can render is not in the lobby but in the debate. They can ask the inconvenient question that an official Opposition will never ask.

Until recently it was possible to argue that the two-party system at least gave us a stability of government, that those who ruled the state might not be ruling it democratically but at least they were ruling it sanely. Power was in the hands of men who, in whatever antics they might indulge on secondary matters, could at least be trusted not to behave with such reckless folly as to endanger the existence of the nation. One could point to such a career as that of Ernest Bevin at the Foreign Office in support of such a thesis. But after Suez we can no longer have this confidence in governmental sanity. Who exactly in the Government was in favour of Suez and who merely lacked the courage to say that he was against it, we shall perhaps never know. But at least the whole episode proved that we can no longer take for granted the sanity of our leaders—that it is much too dangerous to leave power without any real possibility of challenge in the hands of the executive, and therefore, at whatever inconvenience, it is necessary to restore the reality of Parliament by breaking the two-party monopoly. But whether there be an Establishment in the sense in which the word is commonly used, I am less sure. The executive has great power and the Civil Service has great power. The vested interests of capital and organized labour have great power. So have the managers, and it is uncertain in any given tug-of-war who will prove to be the victor, but whether there is some mysterious, social influence, independent of them all, which really controls our destinies, I am less certain. There are moments perhaps when one wishes that there was.

The B.B.C.

by Henry Fairlie

Age 35. One of England's few columnists and the first to have used the phrase 'The Establishment'. Now on the *Daily Mail*. Educated at Corpus Christi, Oxford. Married, three children.

OF all the voices of the Establishment, the British Broadcasting Corporation's is the most powerful. Like other institutions of the Establishment, it has taken a knock or two in recent years. But, inexorably, its spirit will triumph. It has, indeed, already triumphed. When a rival organization, the Independent Television Authority, was created its members included Sir Kenneth Clark, Lord Layton, Dr. J. T. Honeyman, the Rector of Glasgow University, and Miss M. E. Popham, a former Principal of Cheltenham Ladies' College. Not one among them but, in another year or so, might have been appointed a governor of the B.B.C. itself; not one that did not represent the 'British mentality at its best', as Reith had insisted that the B.B.C. should do.

Clifford Allen of Hurtwood once wrote to Reith, saying that he was fascinated by the way in which the B.B.C. was creating its own ritual. He was referring to its public ritual, its tireless and solemn celebration of public occasions. A monarch has a birthday, the national anthem is played before the news; one monarch dies, the loudspeakers go silent; another monarch dies, they relay only solemn music. There are even precedents now for handling a monarch's abdication. A State opening of Parliament or a Boy Scout's Jamboree: a great body of conventions has been built up at Broadcasting House for presenting either. Occasionally the liturgy is altered, something added to, or subtracted from, the established formulary; but, even so, it is still the same, as if the B.B.C. was itself part of the ceremony: that crozier, really a microphone; the censer boys, attendant producers; and, beneath that rich cope, Richard Dimbleby himself. It is a significant comment on the confused state of British opinion that, in recent years, the B.B.C. has had no more enthusiastic defenders than the Labour Party, although it has done more than any other body to buttress the most conservative institutions in the country, to create and perpetuate reverence for the orders, the privileges and the mysteries of a conservative society.

But the B.B.C. has created its own ritual inside its own organization, which is just as significant. Part of it is no different from the ritual of any overgrown bureaucracy. As Malcolm Muggeridge has written, the B.B.C. 'came to pass silently, invisibly; like a coral reef, cells multiplying, until it was a vast structure, a conglomeration of studios, offices, cool passages along which many passed to and fro; a society, with its king, lords and commoners, its laws and dossiers and revenue and easily suppressed insurrection.' By the time a new idea has received the benediction of each order of the hierarchy, it has usually ceased to be an idea and become a piece of case-law, binding rather than freeing. It is a wonder, indeed, that in such circumstances the producers at the B.B.C. should ever achieve anything for enterprise or moment, and almost anyone who has ever had anything to do with the B.B.C. will pay a willing tribute to their devotion to their work; it is only by their persistence that what is heard through the loudspeaker is not always muffled, what is seen on the screen is not always sicklied o'er with the pale cast of second thoughts.

The ritual is most easily observed at the level of heads of departments and their assistants. Watch one of them greet an eminent person, a bishop or a Cabinet minister or a trade union leader. The eminent person is ushered into what is, perhaps a little ironically, known as the 'hospitality' room; the head of department, who has never had his eye off the door, bolts the last corner of his sandwich and advances, hand outstretched, an obsequious smile laid across a face which is sallow from days spent in fruitless committees; he breathes the ritual B.B.C. welcome to eminent persons, 'How good of you to come,' and, overcome, relapses into a bold offer of a glass of sherry; if this is the kind of programme in which the eminent person is to be questioned by a number of journalists, the next fifteen minutes are spent in introducing him to his inquisitors, with the smiling, ritual reassurance, 'I don't think you have anything to fear from Mr. ——'; nor does he, for Mr. —— has already had it pointed out to him that the point of the programme is, not to put the eminent person on the spot, but to 'reveal his personality'; after a short run-through, the producer is desperate and takes the opportunity, while the head of department is reassuring the eminent person, to urge the inquisitors to be tough with their victim; but the resources of the B.B.C. are not yet exhausted; the chairman of the discussion has been chosen for a good reason; when the programme is actually on the air, at the precise moment when one more supplementary question would pin the eminent person to at least one clear statement of his opinion, the chairman intervenes with the languid observation, 'I think we have had enough of that question. May I ask, Sir, if it is true that your hobby is fishing?' The full ritual has once more been played through without a hitch; the producer retires, despondent, for a drink round the corner; the head of department assures the eminent person that his personality 'came across well'; and the eminent person withdraws, convinced, as so many before have been, that the B.B.C. is a force for good in the land.

Now, the whole point about this behaviour is that it is born, not just of the timidity of a bureaucracy, but of the natural obsequiousness towards authority of any part of the Establishment. 'Broadcasting', wrote Reith in his autobiography, 'has for long been recognised as an estate of the realm.' It is one of the few unchallengeable statements in the book. The B.B.C. can lay claim to the title of the fourth estate with far more justice than can the Press, which anyhow should never have regarded the title as in any way creditable. What matters is not that the B.B.C. by its constitutional position, is liable to have to submit to pressure from the political authority, although its defenders tend to underestimate the frequency with which such pressure has been exerted. As W. J. M. Mackenzie and J. W. Grove, in their textbook, *Central Administration in Britain*, point out: 'Since the B.B.C, was set up as a public body in 1927, the government has many times intervened in particular matters of day-to-day administration although it has no formal powers to do so. A case in point was the attempt of the B.B.C. to merge its Western and Midland Regions, a proposal which met with such stiff political opposition inside and outside Parliament that the Corporation was forced to abandon it.' Cases of direct intervention such as this are not, however, as important as the assumption that underlies all the B.B.C.'s attitudes to authority: namely, that it *ought* to be on the side of authority.

This assumption was never more clearly stated than by Reith himself, in a letter to Baldwin at the time of the General Strike. 'Assuming,' he wrote, 'the B.B.C. is for the people and that the Government is for the people, it follows that the B.B.C. must be for the Government in this crisis too.' This remarkable assertion, remarkable in its unconscious self-revelation, deserves to stand as the classic definition of the Establishment's attitude to those in positions of power. It is precisely this self-deluding assumption that their own views must correspond with the interests of the whole nation, and the equally strong presumption in favour of the political authority of the day, which are at the root of the Establishment's attitudes. It is not surprising that they should have found their firmest expression in an utterance of the first Director-General of the British Broadcasting Corporation.

The legend of the B.B.C.'s independence and impartiality has been so sedulously spread that it is necessary to expose it at some length. It is possible to do this by taking the evidence almost entirely from the autobiography of Reith himself. This extraordinary book is almost as terrifying as James Hogg's *Confessions of a Justified Sinner*, with which it has a more than coincidental resemblance. Here, for all to see, is a detailed self-description of what happens to a man who can totally persuade himself that all that he does is done in the cause of righteousness. 'I was entirely moral,' he writes of himself at the age of fifteen. Ten years later, he sees himself as a man 'of principle and character and will'. 'It was indeed royal to do good and be abused', he comments at another point. This was the man, impelled by ambition, protected by his arrogance, sustained by an almost inexhaustible capacity for self-deception, who decided to use the new instrument of broadcasting in order to impose on the people what he thought would be good for them. As will be seen, he developed, as he proceeded on his chosen path, an authoritarian philosophy, compounded of an obsessive contempt for ordinary people and an unassailable belief in his own rectitude, which has left a lasting influence far beyond the corridors of Broadcasting House.

In his autobiography, Reith makes much of the fact that the B.B.C was not commandeered by the Government during the General Strike of 1926. (The B.B.C. was not then a public corporation, but it was about to become one.) In spite of this, at no time during the General Strike did the B.B.C. behave either independently of the Government's wishes or impartially towards the strikers. Soon after the strike began, for example, the Archbishop of Canterbury telephoned to Reith personally, saying:

'that a manifesto had been drawn up by the leaders of all the Churches; might he broadcast it? He said that he had already communicated with No. 10 and had been told that the Prime Minister would not prevent its being broadcast, though he would prefer not; he had been told to apply to me. A nice position for me to be in between Premier and Primate; bound mightily to vex one or other. . . .'

As might be expected, the Archbishop's statement was an innocuous one, proposing terms under which the strike might be called off and negotiations opened, whereas Baldwin had stated that he would not discuss terms until the strike had been called off. Reith talked next to J. C. C. Davidson, who was then acting as Deputy Chief Civil Commissioner, who told him:

'categorically that the statement should not be broadcast and that the Prime Minister hoped it would not be. . . . Rightly or wrongly, therefore, I told the Archbishop on the telephone I was sorry the statement could not be broadcast. He said he supposed the Prime Minister had objected. I replied that the responsibility was mine.'

Such was how Reith interpreted the independence of the B.B.C.

But worse was to come. Reith himself suggested to the Prime Minister that he should broadcast to the nation, and Baldwin said that he would like to do so. As if this strange initiative on the part of a supposedly impartial figure were not enough, Reith proceeded to write into Baldwin's manuscript the most famous words which the Prime Minister was to utter during the strike. When Baldwin arrived at Reith's house, he:

'handed me his manuscript. "Tell me what you think of this," he said. I suggested one alteration which he agreed. Then he said he thought of ending with something personal. "Yes," I replied, "something about people trusting you. And what about you saying that you're a man of peace; that you're longing and working and praying for peace; but that you won't compromise the dignity of the constitution?" "Excellent," he said, "write it down if you have a legible hand." I did so. . . .'

Reith's hand was legible enough; a moment later the skilful words were uttered.

This, however, was not all.

'Another embarrassment next day. Ramsay MacDonald telephoned to ask if he might broadcast; he knew I was not entirely a free agent, but might he send along a draft? This he did with a friendly note offering to make alterations. I asked Davidson to show it to the Prime Minister and to say I strongly recommended it should go out. Davidson told me it certainly could not go; it would set Churchill off again.'

Thus, as the result of Reith's ready deference to the expressed wishes of the Government, both the Archbishop of Canterbury and the Leader of the Opposition were banned from the air. It was not until the strike was over that a member of the Labour Party was at last allowed to broadcast.

At the end of the strike came the most remarkable and most ludicrous episode of all. On the evening of the day on which the strike was called off, Reith himself read a message which the Prime Minister had written, again at Reith's request. 'It was,' he records in his autobiography, 'an appeal to forget what had happened, to look forward, to build the country up again.' The sentiment—the 'appeal to forget what had happened'—was true to the mystique of the Establishment. Clearly, something out of the ordinary was demanded by the occasion. Reith found it. Baldwin's message was followed immediately by a reading of Blake's 'Jerusalem', which was then repeated by orchestra and choir.

> *Bring me my bow of burning gold:*
> *Bring me my Arrows of desire:*
> *Bring me my Spear: O clouds unfold:*
> *Bring me my Chariot of fire.*

But what Reith got was a knighthood in the New Year's Honours List.

Two other examples may be given of the deference which the B.B.C. under Reith showed to authority. In 1931, Churchill asked that he should be allowed to broadcast his views on India. Reith suggested that, if this were permitted, someone representative of

the Left wing should be allowed to broadcast as well, and that
these two should be followed by a spokesman of the Round Table
point of view. It was a reasonable proposal, but once again the
Government intervened, and once again the B.B.C. hastily with-
drew:

'We went to see the Secretary of State. He was most appre-
hensive of the effect of such a series of talks at that time; it
would do immense harm in India. The Board (of Governors of
the B.B.C.) decided to accede to the request so emphatically
made by the Minister responsible for dealing with a particularly
delicate and critical situation. One does not need to endorse his
attitude and apprehensions to understand the Board's decision.'

Of course, the point is that almost any Minister, at any moment,
can claim that the situation for which he is responsible is 'particularly delicate and critical'. As every journalist knows, it is the
commonest excuse given by a Minister who is trying to prevent
either news or comment being published. The only difference is
that journalists tend to be more sceptical of the excuse than the
B.B.C. proved to be on this occasion.

As is well known, Churchill was kept off the air during the
whole of the period of German rearmament before the 1939-45
war. Reith makes no mention of this in his 500 pages of autobiography, although it was a decision which even his successor as
Director-General of the B.B.C., W. J. Haley, concedes to have
been 'not so admirable'. Reith may not have been ultimately
responsible for the banning of Churchill—it was due partly to an
agreement with the major parties, under which political broad-
casters were nominated by the party Whips; and partly to the
presumption in favour of established authority which has been
shown by every Board of Governors of the B.B.C.—but his silence
must be taken to mean that throughout the years from 1933 to
1939 he never demurred.

In June, 1932, Reith played a characteristic role in ensuring
the maximum publicity for the plans of the Government:

'On Monday, June 27, I was informed that the Chancellor,
Neville Chamberlain, had decided to convert the £2,000 million
War Loan from five to three and a half per cent. The Cabinet

were not to hear about it until 9 p.m. on the following Thursday; he wanted the widest and most intelligent publicity; I was asked to suggest the means.

The Prince of Wales was to broadcast from a Canadian dinner at 9.35 that night; it was arranged that at the end of his speech he should say that the Chancellor was just going to make an important announcement in the House of Commons and warn people to listen to their wireless thereafter. The Chancellor's speech would be given to me on Thursday afternoon and it would be broadcast immediately he had spoken in the House. . . . It went off all right.'

Such was the part played by Reith in establishing the supposed independence and impartiality of the B.B.C. Like many Scotsmen and most sons of the manse, Reith was always 'deeply respectful towards those set in authority over him and expecting a corresponding respect from those over whom he was set.' It was this attitude of mind which he instilled into the B.B.C from the moment of its birth, and the B.B.C. is not rid of it yet.

It may be objected that Reith left the B.B.C. as long ago as 1938, and that the evidence of more than twenty years ago is no longer necessarily relevant today. There is some slight truth in this. Haley, the only other remarkable Director-General whom the B.B.C. has known, made many changes, and he certainly freed the B.B.C. from many of its formal entanglements with the major parties. The Whips no longer have a stranglehold on political broadcasting, although their influence is still formidable enough. But there is no evidence that Haley in any way changed the B.B.C.'s fundamental attitude to those in authority. No full or relevant memoirs of the period following Reith have yet been published, and this makes it difficult to offer documented examples of the B.B.C.'s behaviour, without falling back on unsupported, or unpublishable, verbal evidence or on the necessarily suspect accounts of those who have quarrelled with the Corporation. But, in fact, the conduct of the B.B.C. at critical or awkward moments speaks for itself. When, it is pertinent to ask, has a strike leader been offered facilities by the B.B.C. similar to those which were given to Eden during the national railway strike of 1955? Why ban the second of two scheduled interviews merely because in the first Siobhan McKenna made a few spritely observations about the

Northern Ireland Government? The examples could be multiplied. The B.B.C remains today as deferential to those in authority and as predisposed in their favour as ever Reith could have wished that it be. It allows fair play only when the two front benches are agreed about a policy, and then only to the front-bench point of view. This belief in bi-partisanship, as will be shown, has its source in instincts far more complicated than the simple desire to play safe.

Few activities of the B.B.C. encourage this attitude to authority more subtly and more persistently than its news broadcasts. These are, it is claimed, impartial, accurate and trustworthy. They are, in fact, nothing of the sort. A pointed description of a B.B.C. news bulletin may be found in a letter which Jennie Flexner wrote to Tom Jones in 1938. Writing from New York, she said:

'It has been interesting to hear what the B.B.C. sends us: great detail about the English weather; quite full information about the U.S.A. culled from our commentators; and then a little carefully arranged news about Europe in general. So the *New Statesman* is very welcome and we thank you very much.'

She was describing an oversea news bulletin in 1938; a home news bulletin twenty years later is little different. A journalist, listening to such a bulletin, is impelled to ask himself whether it bears any relation to the search for news on which he has been engaged during the day, whether for *The Times* or the *Daily Mirror*. The answer can only be that it does not. A B.B.C. news bulletin may sometimes give facts; it only rarely gives news; and it scarcely ever gives the truth of an event or a situation.

This is partly due to its own peculiar conception of what constitutes news. One may take a typical example. A Minister, as is often the case, introduces a Bill which has been forced on him by party or public pressure, but every political correspondent knows, because he has been informed, that the Government's legislative programme is to be so arranged that it will never reach the statute book, and this fact is reported in most newspapers. What does the B.B.C. do? It reports the fact that the Bill is to be introduced; it does not, however, report the equally significant fact, which necessarily alters the first, that the Bill will be strangled and that its introduction has merely been a familiar and time-honoured political manœuvre. Examples such as this occur almost every day. By divorcing a happening from its origins and its circumstances, the B.B.C. in its news bulletins is as guilty of a gross distortion of fact and truth as any politically biased newspaper, and almost certainly more consistently so.

But the manner in which the B.B.C. presents the news holds more serious dangers than that. In its selection of news, in its careful phrase and in its unspeakable diction, it fosters the illusion that in every public issue there is a body of ascertainable fact, on which a rational man may found a rational opinion. This is a perilous delusion, especially if people come to believe that the ascertainable fact is unfailingly communicated to them by one body, the B.B.C. It is far preferable that public issues should be presented as they are in the Press, as collisions of great interests, prejudices and appetites; and if these sometimes appear unattractive, it is right that they should do so, for unattractive they frequently are. It is far preferable that the fears and appetites of trade unionists or stockbrokers should be plainly represented and plainly recognizable in the *Daily Herald* or the *Daily Telegraph* than that they should be given respectability and innocence by a B.B.C. news editor and a B.B.C. announcer.

A further danger is that, by its selection of news, the B.B.C. gives the impression that political decisions are taken by a few great and remote men for reasons which are never, can never and should never be explained. Kruschev makes a speech, Adenauer forces a *démarche*, de Gaulle sends a protest: all of them come as mysteriously from the blue and end as mysteriously in the blue as any titbit of information which filtered out of the chancelleries of Metternich's Europe. Politics, according to the B.B.C. news bulletins, is a matter for those set in authority, and the doings of those set in authority are reported without partiality or favour: without partiality or favour, that is, except to those set in authority. The attitudes of the dissident or the nonconformist, even the common-sense evaluations of ordinary people, find no place in a B.B.C. news broadcast; or, if they do find a place, it is as a peremptory postcript to the elaborate, and even affectionate, accounts of the to-ings and fro-ings of the lords of the universe.

Now, it is not claimed that these dangers are due entirely to any deliberate policy of the B.B.C. In the first place, a B.B.C. news bulletin is limited, at the most, to fifteen minutes, which represents less than two columns of *The Times*. This makes it unavoidable that much will be omitted for which a newspaper can find room, especially since the B.B.C., observing its own order of priorities, considers it necessary to repeat at length almost every official pronouncement or communique and to record in detail the otiose routine of even semi-attached royalty. But even more important is the fact that the B.B.C., in constructing its news bulletins, is guided by no sense of news values. It is not sufficiently appreciated that one of the casual protections which a free press gives to its public is simply the news sense of its editors, news editors and night news editors. Precisely because they are, first and last, interested in what will interest their readers, they from time to time give prominence to news and views which the B.B.C. would either ignore or bury in the middle of its bulletins. This news sense is not infallible; it is often distorted; the trivial is frequently elevated, the significant sometimes over-looked. But, by and large, the press is far more likely than the B.B.C. to stumble on the significant, especially the significant which is uncomfortable to authority, and present it in such a way that it cannot be ignored: to stumble on it, if one likes, primarily out of an instinct for sensation.

But the criticism of the B.B.C.'s attitude to news which embraces all the others is that it does not attempt to discover the truth. It merely records public events and public statements. Not for it to investigate on its own account the accusations against the Thurso police and decide that they deserve to be ventilated; it must wait until officialdom has admitted that they are a public issue. Not for it to make its own inquiry into the massacre at Hola Camp and present its own findings; it is satisfied with repeating official pronouncements. Not for it to unearth some public scandal, such as the Electrical Trades Union's disposal of its funds; it will ignore the subject until authority has given its official licence to publish. Thus, even in its news bulletins, in that part of its activities which is most commonly and widely praised, the B.B.C. is dependent on authority. It is to authority that it looks for guidance in its selection of news, instead of to a fallible but free news sense; and it is from authority that it takes the tone which informs all its news bulletins. Fed by authority, it is to authority that it gives homage.

But the attitude of the B.B.C. towards those in power is not the most interesting of its characteristics and certainly not the most relevant in a discussion of the Establishment. The Establishment is a difficult and, if misunderstood, dangerous conception. It is a pity, one sometimes feels, that it was ever popularized and there is much to be said for the view that it should have been left to ferment in the more obscure vats of A. J. P. Taylor's writings.

Intended to assist inquiry and thought, this virtuous, almost demure, phrase has been debauched by the whole tribe of professional publicists and vulgarizers who today imagine that a little ill-will entitles them to comment on public affairs. Corrupted by them, the Establishment is now a harlot of a phrase. It is used indiscriminately by dons, novelists, playwrights, poets, composers, artists, actors, dramatic critics, literary critics, script-writers, even band leaders and antique dealers, merely to denote those in positions of power whom they happen to dislike most. If this is all that the Establishment means, the phrase is unnecessary and a fraud. It is necessary and valuable only if it helps to describe something specific about the manner in which power in England is exercised, something that has been previously overlooked or insufficiently examined. In this limited object, the conception of the Establishment can be of some assistance. But although it may be possible to rescue the idea of the Establishment from prostitution, there is no promise that a respectable woman can be made of the Establishment itself. Even General Booth had to admit that there were tasks beyond his powers.

The idea of the Establishment is concerned less with the actual exercise of power than with the established bodies of prevailing opinion which powerfully, and not always openly, influence its exercise. The Establishment is not a power *élite*. If its members have any connexions with power blocs in society, it is not these connexions which give them their particular influence. If in their other activities they represent actual interests, it is not their representation of these interests which makes them members of the Establishment. Indeed, the one significant fact about the Establishment is that it represents nothing in the national life. It has its roots in no class and no interest; it responds to no deep-seated national instinct. It is this rootlessness which is seen by its defenders as its main virtue, and by its opponents as its most depressing fault. Its defenders have, of course, found a euphemism for this rootlessness: they call it disinterestedness. It must be disinterested, they argue, precisely because it represents nothing. What, after all, has the Warden of All Souls to gain? He is retained by no industry. He receives little or no emolument for his untolled services. No higher academic honour can fall to a man who must already be surprised at the full recognition of his talents. Where find a more disinterested or impartial person? Where, indeed, unless in the twilit figure of a still surviving Liberal or a retired Civil servant or a pale headmaster. All of these, it need scarcely be pointed out, are usually to be found in any Board of Governors of the B.B.C., which, however composed, may confidently be taken as a microcosm of the Establishment of the day. They move in a world which is utterly separated from reality, governed only by its own mystique. Deprived of real experience, impelled by no real interest, avoiding any real conflict, it is to this, the exalted representation of nothing that they would like to reduce the social and political life of Britain.

Nothing, of course, could be more seductive. The representation of nothing can only be replaced by the representation of something: by the representation of specific interests, which may mean conflicting interests, or of real ideas, which may mean conflicting ideas. How much more simple, how much more civilized, to avoid painful decisions, to represent nothing, to be nothing. The Left-wing critics of the Establishment have altogether missed this vital point. If the Establishment represented established interests, it might, from their point of view, still be deserving of criticism. But why create a new term to describe power blocs which are already familiar? The whole point about the Establishment is that it represents no interests; and its claim to disinterestedness may, in this sense, be readily accepted.

One clear, and relevant, example of this may be given. In the long discussion which preceded the introduction of commercial television, the Establishment came as near as it has ever done to organising a campaign against the Government of the day, a Conservative Government. The earnest periods of Vice-Chancellors writing to *The Times;* the grim tenacity of Lady Violet Bonham Carter; the lengthy judgement of a Lord of Appeal in Ordinary, Lord Radcliffe, who actually wrote a letter to *The Times* which occupied one whole column; the soft, enfolding, platitudes of the Archbishop of Canterbury; the persistent lobbying of W. J. Haley: not a step was omitted. The debate on commercial television remains one of the clearest examples of the Establishment in action in defence of one of its dearest illusions, namely, that it knows best what is good for other people. But the significant fact to observe is that the Establishment was at this point opposed to a Conservative Government and to the numerous business interests which advocated the introduction of commercial television. Why the Establishment should regard the defence of the B.B.C.'s monopoly as so essential to its own preservation is in itself significant; and in the rest of this essay an attempt will be made to trace the answer.

What makes the influence of the B.B.C. on the life and mind of the nation so baleful is the wash of 'gentle persuasion', as Muggeridge described it twenty years ago, 'patiently wearing away angular opinions; like waves on a beach, ebbing and flowing, transforming rocks and stones into smooth round pebbles, all alike. . . .' This is its true mission. It fears, and when it does not fear it despises, non-conformity; and, if non-conformity must be allowed its say, it will gently rob it of all anger and all laughter, of all passion and all heartache, until it lacks both pith and point. Aneurin Bevan, in *In Place of Fear*, describes how a new member of the House of Commons, imagining that he has thrown a brick at the members opposite, finds to his bewilderment that it has turned into a sponge in mid-air. Much the same alchemy is practised by the B.B.C.

It is most evident in discussions. The point of these discussions, as anyone who has listened to them knows but those who have taken part in them know even better, is not to find and explore the point of difference, but to find and scrupulously to map the common area of agreement. In these discussions, the chairmen are all-important, and one sometimes wonders if the B.B.C. does not breed them especially for the purpose in a B.B.C. Hatchery and Conditioning Centre, for it is difficult to believe that they were born of viviparous parents. 'Well, well, well,' says one, when two members of his team have for once been aroused, 'they did get excited about that, didn't they?' The audience laughs and is soothed. 'I am afraid,' says another, 'that the team cannot agree about that. Let's hurry on to the next question.' His pain and surprise at such a default are barely concealed. More commonly, however, even when a discussion has just concluded between three or four people of immovably opposed points of view, the chairman will sum up with bland indifference to what has been said in the preceding half-hour, rescuing from a wide area of conflict some small patch of common agreement which he can offer to the listeners as their reward for hearing him out.

Now, all this is not just an accident, nor does it spring just from a desire to play safe, discreditable enough though this motive would be in itself. It has its origin in the attitude which those in possession and in power try sedulously to foster among those who do not possess and do not have power, the attitude which is common to the B.B.C. and to the Establishment. It is difficult, in these days, to persuade a majority of people to accept ideas merely because they are advanced by authority or prescribed by custom. It is far easier and more effective to persuade them that there really is no difference between apparently opposing points of view, that there really is no conflict either of ideas or interests with which they need bother their heads, that there really is nothing worth getting excited about. Here is the real danger of the B.B.C. It does not preach; it does not even try to persuade; it brainwashes, and it brainwashes with such skill that no one notices. This is its value to the Establishment. It would turn up its nose at subliminal advertising. But it is guilty, day in and day out, of subliminal advocacy, slipping in, through the apparently innocuous words of the chairman, a whole attitude to life and thought.

No attitudes exist in isolation, and it is important to the Establishment that it should encourage acceptance of prevailing opinion in all fields of thought and art. To this task, the B.B.C. brings conviction as well as other qualities. It is in its nature that it should find thinkers or artists acceptable to it only when they have become generally accepted. It hunts names, experts and accepted authorities. Its guide to the world of thought, letters and the arts is *Who's Who;* its list of Reith lecturers might have been culled from *Who Was Who*. 'A statesman is a dead politician', runs the apophthegm; a Reith lecturer is a dead thinker. Where the boundaries of accepted thought are being crossed, there you will not find the B.B.C.; where there is dissidence or protest, there you will not find the B.B.C.; where there is irreverence or resistance to cant, there you will not find the B.B.C. For a body such as the Royal Academy, there is point in its conservatism; its task is to inform and discipline every new development with tradition. But for the B.B.C.'s attitude there can be no defence. It is not even conservative; it is certainly not the repository of a traditional discipline. It moves sluggishly with all that is worst in British life, all that finds prevailing opinion safe and comforting.

A recent example is the introduction, on B.B.C. television, of a supposedly highbrow programme called *Monitor*. Fortnight by fortnight, the painters, sculptors, poets, composers, film directors and playwrights who are generally accepted are brought before the cameras, The standard of acceptance is, of course, simple. It is success. Corbusier, Robert Graves, Betjeman, Bernstein of the New York Philharmonic Orchestra: they are all introduced to the gaping British public now, but how many of them would have been introduced before they were successful. Would Corbusier have been treated with such reverence thirty years ago? Would Betjeman have been dragged, with apparently no show of reluctance, from his private haunts, if his book of poems had not just become a best-seller, and a prize been presented to him by Princess Margaret? The programme is, perhaps, the most dishonest and obscene that the B.B.C. carries, but its underlying assumptions pervade the whole of the B.B.C.'s attitude to thought and the arts. It is dis-honest, because it pretends to honest standards of judgement; obscene because it finds virtue in standards of success which bear little relation to the actual virtue of the work itself.

The relevance of this to the Establishment has already been hinted. Protest never comes from one quarter alone. The effective protest may well lie in some activity which seems far removed from public affairs. It is therefore essential to it that it should ensure, as far as possible, that in every field of ideas only those which are acceptable to it are given prominence. It does not require a con-ervative institution, because conservatism is a positive attitude and might at times be indefensible; certainly it might well entangle it in a position from which it would find it hard to extricate itself, and the precondition of the Establishment's survival is that it should be able easily to shift its ground with prevailing opinion and so control it. Nor does it want an institution which is so progressive that it entertains protest; that would be to destroy itself. It wants what the B.B.C. provides: an institution which represents all in the life of the nation to which mediocrity has paid the tribute of success and acceptance. Success and conformity:

these are the twins which the Establishment and the B.B.C. labour to uphold.

It may be asked whether a medium of mass communication can be anything but a mirror of prevailing opinion. The answer is that it can, but only on one condition: that one trusts the people to find their way, at will and by their own taste, to attitudes which truly reflect their own yearnings and those of society in which they live. This the Establishment, but in particular the B.B.C., will never allow them to do. It has already been observed that one of the most patient illusions of the Establishment is its belief that it knows best what is good for other people, and the B.B.C. holds the same belief as a legacy from Reith. 'In earliest years', he wrote in his autobiography, 'accused of setting out to give the public not what it wanted but what the B.B.C. thought it should have, the answer was that few knew what they wanted, fewer what they needed.' The result of this attitude was a policy which has been succinctly described by Haley in the Lewis Fry Memorial Lecture which he gave in Bristol University eleven years ago, while he was still Director-General of the B.B.C.:

'The listener was deliberately plunged from one extreme to the other. The devotees of Irving Berlin were suddenly confronted with Bach. Many listeners were won for higher things in this way, but many were irretrievably lost. For the weakness of the process was that so many intolerances were set up.'

Haley went on to describe the policy which he substituted for Reith's:

'Since the war we have been feeling our way along a more indirect approach. It rests on the conception of the community as a broadly based cultural pyramid slowly aspiring upwards. This pyramid is served by three main Programmes, differentiated but broadly overlapping in levels and interests, each programme leading on to the other, the listener being induced through the years increasingly to discriminate in favour of the things that are more worthwhile. . . . As the standards of the education and culture of the community rise so should the programme pyramid also.'

The reverse, of course, has happened. The Third Programme has a much smaller audience than it had at its inception; the Home Service has lowered its standards; and the Light Programme has become unvaryingly banal. The B.B.C.'s television service falls somewhere between the Home Service and the Light Programme.

The element which is common to both Reith's and Haley's attitude is their belief that culture is something which can be transmitted to the mass of a population by a curriculum of humane studies. Their motives were almost certainly different. Reith, a Calvinist to the core, wished to punish people. He wished to give people six of the best every day, and a round dozen on the Sabbath. Haley, a largely self-educated man and in this an almost nineteenth-century figure, believed that people would be enticed, as he was by Benn's Popular Library and Everyman's Library, into voluntarily taking a sort of adult education course through the B.B.C. But, whatever their motives, their fallacy is the same. The mass of a people must find its culture, if it is to be real to them at all, by following their own tastes and their own pleasures.

This is what the B.B.C. have always sought to deny them, and what the Establishment sought to deny them by resisting the introduction of commercial television. One can scarcely blame it. Its one hope of maintaining its position is to devitalize the people, to insinuate its own standards of success and mediocrity, to impose its own culture and with it its own attitudes, until they think and feel with it. The Establishment knows that a population with independent tastes, even if its tastes are only Tommy Steele and Terry Dene, is a population which is capable of feeling, thinking, and therefore perhaps even acting, independently of it. A population which can erect its own idols, even if they are only the idols of Wembley, is a population which will not be pre-disposed to idolize those whom the Establishment would wish it to. It is far safer to brainwash the mass of the population in a middling, middlebrow, middle-class culture; and it is the task of brainwashing an entire population which the Establishment entrusts to the B.B.C. It can entrust it in the full confidence that the B.B.C. will, of its own nature, perform the task to the best of its ability.